POLAND'S POST-WAR DYNAMIC OF MIGRATION

To my little son Mareczek

Poland's Post-War Dynamic of Migration

KRYSTYNA IGLICKA
*Institute for Social Studies,
Warsaw University, Poland*

LONDON AND NEW YORK

First published 2001 by Ashgate Publishing

Reissued 2019 by Routledge
2 Park Square, Milton Park, Abingdon, Oxon, OX14 4RN
52 Vanderbilt Avenue, New York, NY 10017

Routledge is an imprint of the Taylor & Francis Group, an informa business

© Krystyna Iglicka 2001

All rights reserved. No part of this book may be reprinted or reproduced or utilised in any form or by any electronic, mechanical, or other means, now known or hereafter invented, including photocopying and recording, or in any information storage or retrieval system, without permission in writing from the publishers.

Notice:
Product or corporate names may be trademarks or registered trademarks, and are used only for identification and explanation without intent to infringe.

Publisher's Note
The publisher has gone to great lengths to ensure the quality of this reprint but points out that some imperfections in the original copies may be apparent.

Disclaimer
The publisher has made every effort to trace copyright holders and welcomes correspondence from those they have been unable to contact.

A Library of Congress record exists under LC control number:

ISBN 13: 978-1-138-72656-7 (hbk)
ISBN 13: 978-0-367-18942-6 (pbk)
ISBN 13: 978-1-315-19130-0 (ebk)

Contents

List of Figures VII
List of Tables IX
Preface XI
Acknowledgements XIII
List of Abbreviations XV

1 Introduction 1

2 Patterns of Emigration 13
   Introduction 13
   Years 1945-1960 16
   Years 1960-1980 20
   Emigration During the 1980s 24
   Emigration During the Transition Period (1990s) 28
   Survey: General Framework and Methodology 34
      Survey Findings – Strategies of International Mobility 36
      Conclusions 41
   Mechanisms of Income-Generating Migration Before and During the Transition Period 42
      Southern European Countries – New Destination Areas 47
      Conclusions 50

3 Mobility from Poland's East 55
   Introduction 55
   Definition, Statistics and the Scope of the Phenomenon 56
   Survey Results 65

4 Patterns of Immigration 73
   Definition, Statistics and the Scope of the Phenomenon 73
   Channelling the Flux – from *Primitive Mobility* to Migration from the East 75
   Survey Results 88
   Formation of Immigrants' Groups 92

    Ethnic Division on Emerging Foreign Labour Markets 94
        Conceptual Framework 94
        Flux from the East 96
        Flux from the West 101
        Conclusions 105
    Return Migration from the West 106

5   Summary 119

Bibliography 135
Index 143

List of Figures

1.1	A system framework of international migration	3
2.1	Emigration from Poland, 1950-1998	29
2.2	Emigration by age and sex in 1997	30
2.3	Emigration by age, sex and place of residence in 1997	31
2.4	Emigrants (15+) by two extreme educational categories	31
2.5	Share of different types of migrants, whole territory	39
3.1	Trends in emigration and immigration, Poland 1950-1998	56
3.2	Border crossings on the eastern border, 1990-1998	59
3.3	Respondents by nationality	66
3.4	Respondents who would like to work in Western Europe by sex and age	67
3.5	Respondents who would like to live in Western Europe by sex and age	68
4.1	Flow of immigrants, 1950-1998	73
4.2	Decisions on permanent residence permit (PRP) in Poland in the period 1993-1996 taken at the first instance	78
4.3	Asylum seekers by main countries of citizenship (including accompanying family members), 1992-1999	85
4.4	Decisions on refugee claims in Poland, 1993-1998	86
4.5a	Work permits granted individually by branch of economic activity (main countries of origin) – Agriculture and Forestry, 1995-1996	98
4.5b	Work permits granted individually by branch of economic activity (main countries of origin) – Construction, 1995-1996	98
4.5c	Work permits granted individually by branch of economic activity (main countries of origin) – Industry and Transportation, 1995-1996	99
4.5d	Work permits granted individually by branch of economic activity (main countries of origin) – Trade and Catering, 1995-1996	99
4.5e	Work permits granted individually by branch of economic activity (main countries of origin) – Education, 1995-1996	102
4.6	Emigrants and immigrants by educational attainment in Poland, 1996	102

List of Tables

1.1	General characterisation of international migration trends, central and eastern Europe and Soviet Union (successor states), early 1990s	6
2.1	Three types of international migrants	14
2.2	Emigration to Israel, 1955-1960	19
2.3	Emigration from Poland by main countries of destination, 1955-1960	19
2.4	Emigration from Poland by main countries of destination, 1960-1970	21
2.5	Emigration from Poland by sending areas and destination country, 1966-1970	22
2.6	Emigrants from Poland in USA and Canada, 1950-1980	22
2.7	Emigration from Poland to Germany, 1980-1985	27
2.8	Emigrants by sex, 1981-1998	29
2.9	Emigration from Poland by the main countries of destination, 1981-1998	32
2.10	Emigration of ethnic German *Aussiedler*, central and eastern Europe and the Soviet Union, 1950-1994	33
2.11	Operational definitions of migrants types using the household survey data, 1994-1995	37
2.12	Predominant type of migration by commune of origin, 1994-1995	38
2.13	Migrants from each of the communes sampled by the first migration destination, 1994-1995	40
2.14	Settler migrants from each of the communes sampled by the country of destination, 1994-1995	41
2.15	Legal migrants by major destination, Poland, 1981-1992	42
2.16	Illegal net emigrants by major country of destination, Poland, 1 April 1981 to 31 December 1988	43
3.1	Departure of Poles and arrivals of foreigners, 1985-1998	58
3.2	The value of expenditures made by foreigners from neighbouring states in Poland, 1994-1996	60
3.3	Purchases made by foreigners at the Polish Bazaars	61

3.4	Trafficked foreigners detained on the borders (major national groups), 1995-1996	63
3.5	Decisions on expulsion of foreigners taken by district administration by country of origin. Poland: 1994-1998	64
3.6	Respondents according to reason for coming to Poland	69
3.7	Respondents according to plans for remaining in Poland	69
4.1	Immigration to Poland, by country or continent of origin, 1988-1992	74
4.2	Visas with work permit granted in 1994-1998 by most numerous nationalities	76
4.3a	Foreigners granted the permanent residence permit (PRP) in Poland according to the most numerous nationalities, 1993-1997	76
4.3b	Foreigners granted the permanent residence permit (PRP) in Poland according to the most numerous nationalities, 1998-1999	77
4.4	Total marriages contracted according to the spouses' nationality. Poland: 1990-1998	81
4.5	Mixed marriages, 1990-1998 (selected years)	82
4.6	Cases of disappearance or leaving the national territory during the asylum procedure in selected CEEs, 1995-1997	86
4.7	Structure of two migrant groups according to citizenship	89
4.8	Structure of two migrant groups according to family relations in Poland	90
4.9	Structure of two migrant groups according to reason for coming to Poland	91
4.10	Structure of two migrant groups according to plans for remaining in Poland	92
4.11	Work permits for foreigners from Eastern Europe according to type of work, 1994 and 1995	97
4.12	Work permits granted individually by ownership of enterprise (eight top countries of origin) in 1995 and 1996	100
4.13	Work permits for foreigners from Western Europe and the US according to type of work, 1994 and 1995	103
4.14	Permanent departure from the United States to Poland, 1920-1957	107
4.15	Immigration to Poland, 1960-1999	108

Preface

Issues around human migratory movements in Central and Eastern Europe in the post-war era are a topic that has been seldom addressed and insufficiently studied by researchers from both the region itself and from Western Europe.

The few attempts that have been made to make analyses of some depth have mostly centred on post-1989 migratory movements. This is somewhat understandable because only since the fall of the Berlin wall have Western European politicians and societies become aware that the "other," or Eastern, half of Europe, along with its significantly more mobile residents, is inevitably going to approach them economically, commercially, socially, politically and culturally. The opening up of borders brought rejoicing only at the beginning: after a short celebration of all people's freedom of movement, a fear of mass immigration from Central and Eastern Europe overpowered liberal views on freedom of cross-border movement for all European denizens.

A similar fear was echoed in Central European countries. Rapidly growing migration from the "East" during the transformation period led to a strengthening of opinion against the inflow of immigrants. Moreover, at the initiation of talks on the entrance of Central European countries into the European Union, it was made clear that the borders of the new, future Europe that would run along the Bug river between Poland and the former Soviet Union, are to be guarded as stringently, if not more so, as the present border along the Oder river. If ever Europe was simultaneously united and divided it is now, as it shall remain in the near future.

Poland has an exceptionally important role to play from the perspective of a unifying Europe, since the Eastern border of Poland will be (following Poland's ascension to the European Union) the future frontier of the expanded Europe. That is why this work's analysis of the mechanisms behind recent fluxes into Poland of people who, after EU enlargement, would otherwise be excluded from the expanded Europe represents interesting material that is new to the English-language literature.

This book also contains an analysis of Poland-bound migratory movements from the West. An analysis of international migration flows stemming from the penetration of capitalist economic relations into adjacent countries wherein non-market or pre-market social and economic structures prevail was undertaken for the first time in the literature on Eastern European population movements.

This volume fills a gap in the literature as it attempts to make a deep, socio-economic and political analysis of the trends and mechanisms of migration in Central and Eastern Europe (and especially in Poland) since 1945 and in light of future EU expansion. The author emphasises that one should not analyse trends that have occurred after 1989 without being aware of the history and mechanisms behind migratory movements in Central and Eastern Europe prior to that date. That is also why, although changes in patterns and mechanisms of migration that occurred since the collapse of the communist system have been emphasised, the years between 1945 and 1989 act as the reference point for the analysis.

Trends and mechanisms in migration to and from Poland, which is treated as an illustrative country for the whole Central European region, have been analysed according to new approaches in migration theory, approaches that have already been tested for other regions. Having been conducted in such a way, the analysis clearly shows that the "historical perspective" in studying migration movement dynamics is uncommonly productive when examining Poland. Thanks to this perspective, it was possible to indicate why and how Poland, a central European latecomer to the global stage, has slowly begun to change from being a major sending country into being a country of net-immigration and transit. The historical perspective has also helped to show and analyse Poland's slow transformation from a country belonging to the Central and Eastern European migration system into a country that soon may belong simultaneously to two otherwise separate ones: the Eastern and the Western European systems.

Acknowledgements

I managed to write this book thanks to many people who at different times were present in my life. Firstly, I would like to thank my mum, whose life and attitudes made me aware that in order to achieve her professional goals a woman must be extremely dynamic and strong. Secondly, I would like to express my gratitude to the late Keith Sword, who taught me self-confidence and firmness at the time he worked with me in the years 1996-1998. I would also like to thank my family (my husband and my son), who due to my ambitions and commitments related to my job for many years bravely endured numerous moves, life in different countries and continents, and sometimes many months of separation. Finally, I wouldn't have been able to write this book if not for my Fulbright scholarship which enabled me to spend a time in the Population Studies Center at the University of Pennsylvania in 1999/2000. I am highly indebted to the Board of Directors of the Polish-American Fulbright Commission who nominated me for this scholarship and to Doug Massey for his kindness and assistance.

List of Abbreviations

CEE – Central and Eastern Europe
CIM – the German Public Recruitment Agency for Highly Skilled Professionals
CIS – Commonwealth of Independent States
CMEA – Council of Mutual Economic Assistance
CoE – Council of Europe
COMECON – see CMEA
CSO – Central Statistical Office
EU – European Union
FRG – Federal Republic of Germany
FYROM – Former Yugoslav Republic of Macedonia
GDR – German Democratic Republic
GPC – Governmental Population Commission
GRC – German Red Cross
GUS see CSO
ISS UW – Institute for Social Studies, University of Warsaw
KC PZPR – Central Committee of the Polish United Workers' Party
OECD – Organization for Economic Cooperation and Development
OSCE – Organization for Security and Cooperation in Europe
PAU ECE – Population Activity Unit at the Economic Commission for Europe
PCK – Polish Red Cross
PESEL – Central Population Register
PHARE – Poland and Hungary Action for Reconstructing the Economy
PRL – Polish People's Republic
PRP – Permanent Residence Permit
SERP – Passport Traffic Registration System
UNHCR – United Nations High Commissioner for Refugees
UPA – Ukrainian Guerilla Army
USSR – Union of Socialist Soviet Republics

1 Introduction

Writing about international migration as it affects the territory of a given country is an extremely challenging and difficult task. It involves writing not only about the population flows from and into that country, but also about the country's history, geography, economy, internal and external policies, issues surrounding immigrants' integration or alienation, etc.

Additionally, the theoretical background on migration is rather weak. To date, there is no single general and comprehensive theory of international migration. Existing theories are biased to say the least. Since they have sprung from the different disciplines of geography, sociology, economics and demographics, the stress has been put on different causes and factors in explaining this phenomenon.

For years, researchers analysing international migration relied upon the "pull-push" concept established by Lee (1966). The "push" and "pull" attributes of sending and receiving areas were considered as independent migration variables leading to the migration choices of individuals, households or certain communities. Although never stated explicitly, the nature of the factors considered in the push-pull model have always been exclusively economic. This concept assumed that an equilibrium between forces of economic growth and economic backwardness between different geographic locations was achievable through international migration (Arango, 1998).

In the post-industrial period,[1] however, restrictive migration policies (in pull-push models, they were accounted for merely as an *intervening set of obstacles*), though once virtually absent in the industrial era, have taken on extreme importance. Today, it is the state and its policies that are key-elements in explaining contemporary migration, from both the theoretical and practical perspectives. This fact should be more fully acknowledged and taken into account by either developing new and better models of international migration or trying to build a general theory of this phenomenon.

Indeed, 'it is precisely the control which states exercise over their borders that defines international migration as a distinctive social process' (Zolberg, 1989, p. 405). Although border controls and restrictive policies obviously reduce the flow of immigrants to less than what it would otherwise be, all borders remain permeable to some extent. Undocumented migrants are trafficked or arrive independently and get work in grey economic spheres; other migrants enter through legal exceptions made to otherwise restrictive policies for humanitarian reasons (family reunification, political asylum, natural disasters, temporary refuge, etc). Still others extend their stay, either legally or illegally. In all cases, the size of the actual inflow exceeds that specified by migration policy or that considered necessary by officials and for the public (Arango, 1998).

> In some ways, this state of affairs is highly functional and even adaptive: demand for labour is met by undocumented migrants, 'temporary' workers, and legal immigrants able to overcome the barriers, thereby keeping employers happy, while the government is not perceived as encouraging or promoting immigration, thus avoiding a political backlash. Whether the contemporary nature of immigration is functional or not, the key point is that the dialectics are not so much between the forces of push and pull as between the push and the intervening factors as described by Lee (1966) (Arango, 1998, p. 14).

Widespread dissatisfaction with the pull-push framework and neo-classical economic explanations of the causes behind migration has initiated a serious of new, exciting theoretical approaches such as: new economics of labour migration, dual labour market theory, world system theory, migrants' network theory, etc.[2] For years, research literature on international migration tested theoretical models, trends and patterns of migration in the world's principal migration systems, these being North America, Western Europe, the Gulf region, Asia and the Pacific Rim, and the southern cone of South America.

As Kritz and Zlotnik (1992, pp. 3, 4) write, 'at the basis of the system approach to the study of international migration, there is the concept of a migration system constituted by a group of countries that exchange relatively large numbers of migrants among each other.'

Migration systems can be defined in various ways. The most popular in the literature is a regional approach, a strategy effective inasmuch as geographical proximity is highly correlated with similar cultural and historical backgrounds. Flows of people between the countries belonging to one migratory system occur

> within a national context whose policy, economic, technological, and social dimensions are constantly changing, partly in response to the feedback and adjustments that stem from the migration itself. Population exchanges within the system involve not only permanent migrants, labour migration and/or refugees, but also students, military personnel, businesspeople and even tourists since such short-term movements frequently set the conditions for subsequent long-term ones (Kritz and Zlotnik, 1992, p. 3).

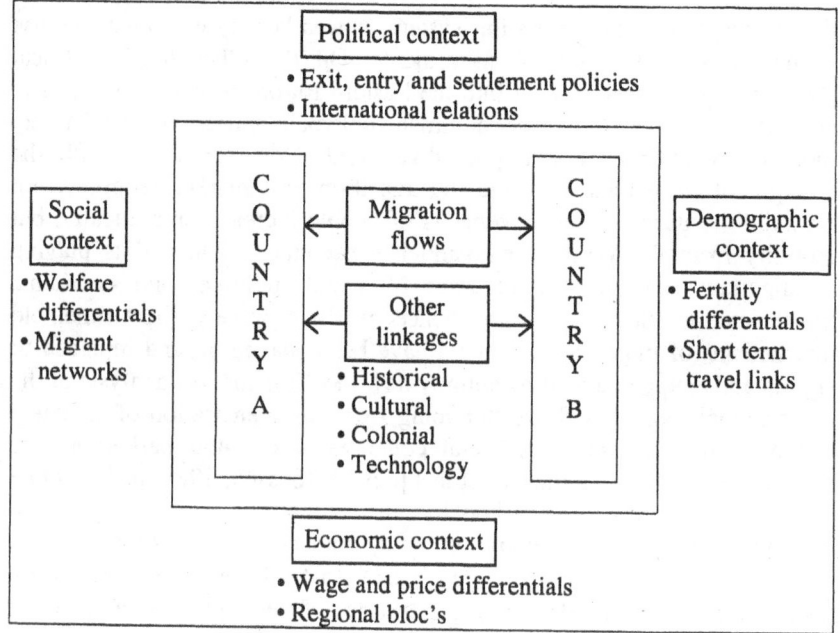

Source: Kritz and Zlotnik, 1992, p. 3

Figure 1.1 A system framework of international migration

* * *

Throughout the past century and a half, central and eastern Europe has mainly been an area of emigration to overseas destination. Subsequently, there was a gradual shift to intra-European migration. A significant proportion of this was regulated, quite successfully, by governments and private institutions. During the Second World War population mobility consisted to a large extend of government-organised resettlement, deportations, forced relocation of labour and refugees' movement. Once the major post-Second World War population transfers had taken place, political reality continued to dominate the forces driving international migration. For the first time in European history emigration restrictions were put in force on a large scale (Frejka, 1996, p. 5).

Poland's geographic and political location predestined it to the struggle and interplay between the West and the East, in both historical and cultural perspectives and economic and social contexts. Although, from the point of view of post-1945 population outflows, Poland gravitated undoubtedly to the Western European migration system, it was largely excluded because of the one-way direction of movements. On the other hand, political circumstances pushed Poland into the Eastern European migration system, since flows between the former communist block countries, albeit relatively moderate were mutual and quite diversified. However, along with the collapse of communist rule and the transition to a market economy, not only did the intra-system movements of people increase dramatically, but mobility from the West into Poland has become visible and is playing an important role in the processes of social, political and economic transformation. Since 1989, and hence over a relatively short time, old mechanisms of migration in Poland have been shaken up and replaced or significantly supplemented by entirely new mechanisms. An analysis of the international migration flows stemming from 'the penetration of capitalist economic relations into peripheral countries where non-market or pre-market social and economic structures prevail' (Sassen, 1988, p. 53) is one of the tasks undertaken in this book.

Due to the restrictive migration policy pursued until 1989 by the states of Central and Eastern Europe (CEE) that shaped both migratory phenomena and knowledge thereof, countries of this region were excluded from the above-mentioned system approach to migration theory-testing. Hardly ever could western researchers analyse the trends and mechanisms of international migration in the CEE region – reliable statistics and other information concerning flows from and to CEE simply did not exist. Furthermore, a majority of researchers from CEE countries did not examine the phenomenon of international migration in the region and towed the communist line of there being no international migration from the communist bloc countries due to the common happiness of their inhabitants. Therefore, the notion of the Central and Eastern European migration system did not even exist in the theoretical and research literature on international migration.

In practice, between 1950 and 1988 international travel in the CEE region was impeded. International population mobility was generally limited to state-controlled settlement emigration related to the process of repatriation of selected ethnic minorities or the strictly controlled mobility of guest workers (usually within the framework of the COMECON) or movements of military personnel (Okolski, 1997).

However, we are now well into a post-industrial, post-Cold War world and about to embark in a brand new century, within which Central and Eastern European latecomers to the global scene will play a crucial role. Therefore, these countries may serve as a model in the theoretical analysis of former, present, emerging and future population movements in Europe.

In the late 1980s and early 1990s, the opening of CEE borders and the disintegration of the former Soviet Union and Yugoslavia fundamentally changed the pattern of migration in the region. When the Berlin Wall came down in November 1989 there was considerable concern in the West about the prospect of an upsurge in east-west migration. As is now well known, the predicted mass migration westwards did not take place. Nonetheless, approximately 2.5 million people did emigrate to the West from the CEECs and the Commonwealth of Independent States (CIS) during the first half of the 1990s. Some of the migratory movements that have occurred in the CEESs during the 1990s are familiar to the international community. Other migratory flows are new to this region such as the flows of transit migrants and the movement of some immigrants on both East-West and West-East axis – a trend, which no one would have expected a decade ago (*Migration in Central and Eastern Europe*, 1999).

After the collapse of the communist regime in 1989, Poland, along with other Central European countries, unexpectedly encountered a number of previously unknown (or seldom experienced) population phenomena. Among these were the massive spatial mobility of citizens of the former USSR, labour migration, from both the East and the West, permanent immigration (mainly from the East), formation of new immigrant communities and the return migration of former émigrés.

The number of persons migrating from the CEE region to the West has fallen substantially since the beginning of the 1990s. Some CEECs have themselves become target countries for an increasing number of economic migrants mainly from their eastern neighbours. However, the full extent of this trend is not recorded by official statistics, given that many of the migrants concerned are engaged in trading and working in the informal economy. In Poland, the largest country in the CEE region, it is estimated that between 100,000-150,000 migrants travel to the country each year to work illegally (*Migration in Central and Eastern Europe*, 1999).

Indeed, it was the combination of migratory pressure from the East, set loose by the collapse of communism, and the restrictive migration policy of Western Europe towards citizens of post-Soviet countries that led to the creation of the Central European buffer zone. Poland is probably the best example of a buffer zone country. From the western perspective, it may also be the most important country since the future of East-West migration to a large degree hinges on Poland's expansion of its visa regime to cover countries of the former Soviet Union.

Table 1.1 General characterisation of international migration trends, central and eastern Europe and Soviet Union (successor states), early 1990s

Country/region	Population 1990 (in millions)	Emigration to:		Immigration
		Other countries In the region	Western countries	
Albania	3.3	Weak (a)	Strong	Weak
Bulgaria	10.0	Weak/transit	Moderate	Weak
Czech Republic	10.4	Weak	Weak	Weak/transit (d)
Hungary	10.6	Weak	Weak	Moderate/transit
Poland	38.2	Weak	Weak	Moderate/transit
Romania	23.2	Moderate/transit	Strong	Weak
Slovakia	5.3	Weak	Weak	Weak
Yugoslavia (successor states)	23.8	Moderate/transit	Strong	Weak
Former USSR				
– Baltic states	8.9	Moderate (b)	Moderate	Weak
– Russian Federation	148.0	Weak	Moderate	Strong
– Other European republics Belarus, Moldova, Ukraine	66.5	Moderate	Moderate	Weak
– Transcaucasian republics	15.9	Strong (c)	Moderate	Weak
– Central Asian republics and Kazakhstan	50.3	Strong	Moderate	Weak

Note: Net emigration per 10,000 population is classified here as (a) 'weak' (below 10), (b) 'moderate' (10-15) and (c) 'strong' (above 15). The characterisation of the other two columns 'emigration to other countries in the region' and 'immigration' is based on a similar approach, but the information is so tenuous that it could not be quantified statistically. The concept 'transit' is mentioned in those cases where transit migration is believed to play a significant role (Frejka, 1996)

Source: UNHCR, Populations of Concern to UNHCR: A Statistical Overview 1993, Geneva, May; reports to UN/ECE by national statistical offices

The key to future East-West European migration lies undoubtedly in the East. More specifically, it lies in the countries of the former Soviet Union. The migration globalisation process will increase the flows from the East inevitably, irrespective of hurdles and restrictive state policies. International flows of people have already started in this part of Europe and all trends are, so far, only increasing. Ten years after the collapse of the communist system, the dynamic process of migration has converted the, formerly temporary, entry of seasonal workers, short-term migrants or refugees from the East into entry with the intention of settlement in Poland. The character and scale of these movements are of considerable significance, not only for politicians and societies in the CEE region but also for European integration. For the foreseeable future, Poland's 1244 km eastern border will remain at least the largest, if not the most important, place where it will still be possible to control East-West pan-European mobility in Europe (Iglicka and Sword, 1999).

> Major trends concerning international movements of the population in the countries of CEE are depicted. In the 1990s, CEE has significantly contributed to the magnitude and diversity of global movements of the population in a striking contrast to what was observed in pre-transition period. Transforming and already rapidly growing economies of CEE have become a magnet for many migrants from outside of the region. Their inflow, combined with remarkably elevated intra-regional mobility of the population of CEE countries seems to fully justify recent references to the region as a new migration pole on the global scene. On the other hand, the diversification of political and economic developments in particular countries of the region led to the emergence of clear sub-regional migration poles within CEE (Okolski, 1998a, p. 11).

One cannot discuss the past and the future of East-West European mobility without discussing the emigration of Poles. For centuries, Polish lands served as one of the biggest sending areas in Europe and a vast reservoir of manpower. One should also not analyse the recent immigration into Poland from the East without considering some implications of this phenomenon for both Poland and the West. Some of the countries of the Central European buffer zone (and Poland among them) will soon be integrated into the Western European migration system. However, fluxes of people on Polish territory, i.e. people who will no longer be excluded in the enlarged Western European migration system, will occur frequently and in different forms. An in-depth understanding of population movements to and from pre-integration Poland should help us to understand future developments. At least this is an aim of this author.

In the 1980s, traditional sending areas of Southern Europe, such as Italy, Spain and Portugal began receiving large numbers of migrants from Africa, Asia and the Middle East. Thus, this part of Europe slowly turned into a net-destination area. The 1990s seem to be Central Europe's turn for changes in migration trends of a similar nature. Although migration balances in the CEECs remain in general negative, i.e. there are still more emigrants than immigrants for most of the CEECs, the gap between emigration and immigration flows is narrowing.

> CEE is a region characterised by temporary labour migration westwards, intra-regional flows of workers, inflows of workers from some developing countries, inflows of highly skilled workers from Western Europe and elsewhere, return migration and ethnic migrations. Superimposed on these types of migration is a complex mosaic of relatively short-term movements based on 'labour tourism' and petty trading and comprising a highly intensive shuttling back and forth across international borders in order to make a living (*Patterns and trends in international migration*, 2000).

Poland is probably the most striking example of a Central European country that is gradually shifting from a major sending area in the region into a country of net-immigration and transit. Analysing the economic and social processes that are behind this transformation represents an appealing task for a researcher and one of the major endeavours undertaken by this author.

This book would appear to be the first attempt for a comprehensive and in-depth combined analysis of the trends and mechanisms of migration from and into Poland since 1945. The emphasis has been put on ongoing changes in migratory patterns and mechanisms that started after the collapse of the political system. However, it is also stressed here that one should not analyse trends that occurred after 1989 without understanding the history and mechanism of migration prior to that date. All trends and mechanisms of migration from and into Poland observed during the transition period are examined here from the perspective of selected, recently-developed theoretical approaches that have already been tested for other migration systems the world over. In that sense, this book fills a gap in the analysis of population movements in Europe.

This volume consists of three chapters plus this introduction and a summary. In chapter two, the patterns of emigration from Poland between the end of the Second World War and 1999 are examined. For the period up to the collapse of the communist system, patterns of emigration are analysed according to the following periodisation: a) 1945 to 1960; b) 1960 to 1980 and c) the 1980s. These were all distinct periods from the ex-Poland's migration point of view. Different causes, mechanisms and patterns of migration occurred in each of them. However, in the opinion of this author, the main determinant of international migration during the communist period was the Polish state policy, which remained restrictive over the whole 1945-1989 period. The author shows that, irrespective of this policy, emigration from Poland (which began on a large scale on Polish lands in the middle of the 19th century) continued through the communist era and caused irreversible changes in the demographic, social and economic character of the country.

The next parts of this chapter are consequently devoted to emigration during the 1990s (a period of great socio-economic transformation). Here, it is shown that the registered outflow from Poland diminished during the transition mainly because of the opportunities for young, urban and well-educated cohorts of Polish society that arose with the social, political and economic transition. These people, up until 1989, had been the most prone to emigrate. The other reason was the introduction by the Polish government of a market-based currency exchange rate. To support this thesis, an analysis of emigration by migrants' main demographic and social traits before and after 1989 has been made.

Unfortunately, this transition also brought economic hardship for other segments of Polish society, such as rural labourers, the blue-collar and the poorly educated, who generally found it difficult to adapt to the requirements of the market economy. This fact is also mirrored in the changes in structures of emigration examined throughout the chapter. Chapter two is based not only on official statistics but also on survey results, which help to understand in-depth mechanisms and changes in the *typos* of migration from Poland. This author introduces here her own typology of migration, one that illustrates clearly the swings in migratory behaviours both before and after the collapse of the communist system. It is stated that, although the outflow from Poland of that period coincided with the liberalisation of the state's foreign travel policy, the outflow also coincided with Western European countries' stricter regulations towards migrant workers and migration based on ethnic affiliation. Thus, during the 1990s external hurdles began to shape migration from Poland. This did not reduce the official (registered) outflow, although it did reduce the unregistered ("illegal") outflow and radically changed Poles' short- and long-term income-generating (economic) migration strategies. Emigration is now decisively more often resorted to maintain the standard of living than to accumulate wealth, buy consumer durables or otherwise enhance one's level of consumption (Iglicka, 2000a).

Besides changes in mechanisms and strategies of the income-generating migration, the author analyses as well changes in the "geography" of this movement, since the destination countries of Poles' short or long-term migration in the 1990s differ strikingly from those in the pre-transition period.

The collapse of the communist system stimulated population movements in the CEE region that were completely unexpected by researchers and policy makers. It caused not only changes in the mechanisms and patterns of outflow from Poland but also resulted in quantitative and qualitative changes in the population inflows (mainly from the East) into Poland. At the beginning of the 1990s, inflows from the East were perceived mainly as a threat to well-established Western European societies, prompting their states to introduce restrictive immigration policies to curtail mobility from the former Soviet Union in putting citizens of that area onto the visa-rule list. It was probably one of the major factors behind the formation of the Central European buffer zone and, in fact, the formation of a new migration system.

In the opinion of this author, the most important outcome of that decision was a massive cross-border mobility of citizens of the former Soviet Union that impacted on the territory of Poland. Chapter three examines mechanisms and patterns of this phenomenon. The author introduces her own terminology and argues that the kind of spatial mobility undertaken by people from the former Soviet Union in Central Europe should be distinguished from other kinds of shuttle movements found elsewhere in the world.

The final part of this chapter is based on the results of several surveys that describe the scope of the *primitive mobility* of people from the former Soviet Union in post-communist Poland. The in-depth mechanisms of this phenomenon are examined, along with its positive and negative social and economic aspects.

Chapter four delves into the patterns of immigration to Poland from both the East and the West. It begins with descriptions of the definitions and categories of immigrants used in official Polish registries. Throughout the chapter, an attempt to present the quantitative scope of flows and ethnicity of foreigners in Poland since 1945 was made. Furthermore, the channels that, along with the development of migrant networks, are converting a part of the *primitive mobility* into long-term or permanent migration into Poland are looked at. The chapter will argue that, because of Western Europe's restrictive migration policy towards citizens of post-Soviet countries, these channels also function to some degree as "a gateway to the West" for some of the immigrants.

Processes that are accompanying Poland's slow shift in status from a country of emigration into a country of net immigration are also covered throughout chapter three. Different categories of immigrants, such as foreigners with permanent residence permits, foreigners with work-permits, temporary residence permit holders, asylum seekers, etc., by country of origin and basic social and demographic traits are examined here. Scenarios for the development of new immigrant communities already in the making in Poland, such as of "new" Ukrainians, of "new" Armenians and of Vietnamese, are also discussed.

The author also reflects on how the changes in Polish legislation, such as the Act of Employment and Counteracting Unemployment (1994), the Constitution of the Republic of Poland (1997) and the Aliens Law (1998), have shaped and influenced the inflows of foreigners into Poland. These acts were created partly as the state's response and adjustment to new migration processes apparent on its territory.

Consecutive sections of chapter four describe the results of a survey on selected immigrant categories in the Warsaw agglomeration and present an in-depth analysis of issues that have come up in Poland due to growing East-West migration, the globalisation of migration and the transformation of the migration system, namely the phenomena of ethnic groups' formation and ethnic divisions on the emerging market for foreign labour. In accordance with one of the theses of this publication, which posits that Poland, as a latecomer to the global stage, may serve as an example and/or model of the changes in population movements under transition circumstances, this author assesses similarities and differences between the immigrants' current situation in Poland and immigrants' roles in Western Europe in the 1970s. She argues that it is too early to speak about problems stemming from the social exclusion of immigrants – one of the biggest social conflicts in Western Europe today. However, she does suggest that conflict between labour and capital will not only will happen but also become one of the most important issues in Poland. This conflict is considered to have been one of the most important social issues in the formative process of immigrants' groups in Western Europe at the beginning of the 1970s. In order to vindicate this argument, the author considers foreigners' situation on labour markets in Poland from the point of view of the dual labour market theory. This approach will help us to understand the economic and social processes that are accompanying the channelling of the fluxes from the East and from the West. It also aids in understanding that the geography of migratory flows into Poland during the transition period pertains to the structure of the global division of labour.

The final section of this chapter examines the phenomenon of the return migration of expatriate Poles and their children from the West, a component of which, classed *a return of innovation* (the return of émigrés who had settled and done economically well abroad), was not visible in Poland during the communist era. Being new, this particular return is considered to be yet another kind of qualitative change in the patterns of migration affecting the territory of Poland. To support this thesis, the results of selected surveys are examined.

Notes

1   The modern history of economic international migration can be divided into four periods: 1) *the mercantile period* – from 1500 to 1800 – in which population mobility (dominated by flows from Europe) was a result of a colonisation process and economic growth under mercantilist capitalism; 2) *the industrial period* – from 1800 till the end of the First World War – when flows from Europe resulting from transformation of the economic structure of this part of the globe and a spread of industrialism to former colonies in the New World were predominant; 3) *the period of limited migration* – from the end of the First World War till the end of the 1950s – during which quite a few immigration-curtailing forces came into play. There were several important receiving countries had passed restrictive immigration laws, the great Depression stopped almost all international movement and the Second World War restrained massive population mobility. The mobility that occurred right after the Second War was of the movement of displaced persons, refugees or expellees and was not related to economic cycles; 4) *post-industrial migration* – arose during the 1960s and is still continuing. During this period, immigration became a truly global phenomenon; the number and variety of both sending and receiving countries increased and Third World countries became a major source of immigrants (Arango, 1998, p. 2).
2   For comprehensive review of the more recent theories of international migration, see Massey et al. (1993).

References

Arango, J. (1998), 'New Migrations, New Theories', in D.S. Massey, J. Arango, G. Hugo, A. Kouaouci, A. Pellegrino and J.E. Taylor (eds), *Worlds in Motion*, Clarendon Press, Oxford.
Frejka, T. (1996), *International Migration in Central and Eastern Europe and the Commonwealth of Independent States*, United Nations, New York and Geneva.
Iglicka, K. (2000a), 'Mechanisms of migration from Poland before and during the transition period', *Journal of Ethnic and Migration Studies*, vol. 26, no. 1, pp. 61-73.
Iglicka, K. and Sword, K. (eds) (1999), *The Challenge of East-West Migration for Poland*, Macmillan, St. Martin's, London, New York.
Kritz, M. and Zlotnik, H. (1992), 'Global Interactions: Migration Systems, Processes and Policies', in M.M. Kritz, L.L. Lim and H. Zlotnik (eds), *International Migration Systems. A Global Approach*, Clarendon Press, Oxford.
Lee, E.S. (1966), 'A Theory of Migration', *Demography*, no. 3, pp. 5-18.
Massey, D.S., et al. (1993), 'Theories of International Migration: Review and Appraisal', *Population and Development Review*, vol. 19, no. 3, pp. 431-65.
Migration in Central and Eastern Europe – Review (1999), IOM, Geneva.
Okolski, M. (1997), New migration trends in Central and Eastern Europe in the 1990s, *ISS Working Papers*, no. 4, Warsaw.
Okolski, M. (1998a), 'Regional dimension of international migration in Central and Eastern Europe', *Genus*, vol. LIV, no. 1-2, pp. 11-37.
Patterns and trends in international migration in Western Europe (2000), Luxembourg, European Commission.
Sassen, S. (1988), *The Mobility of Labor and Capital: A Study of International Investment and labor Flow*, University Press Cambridge, Cambridge.
UNHCR (1993), *Populations of Concern to UNHCR: A Statistical Overview*, Geneva.
Zolberg, A.R. (1989), 'The next waves: migration theory for a changing world', *International Migration Review*, no. 23, pp. 403-30.

2 Patterns of Emigration

Introduction

The object of this chapter is to present the principal factors responsible for international migrations by Poles in the post-war period. It will also attempt to prove that the migration policy of the Polish state was the prime determinant of international migrations from communist Poland.

Poland has been and does remain a country of fairly intensive emigration. For centuries, Polish lands served as a vast reservoir of labour for many countries, most notably for Germany but also for overseas countries settled by Europeans. Sheer numbers were, on one hand, one of the biggest Polish assets, however, they also represented a burden (Iglicka, 2000a). Significant departure waves began between 1860 and 1890 in various regions of partitioned Poland. The major causes of these first migration outflows were the surplus of labour in local agriculture, insufficient demand for workers in local industrial sectors and a relatively high rate of population growth (Pilch and Zgorniak, 1984). It is estimated that, by the outbreak of the First World War, more than 3.5 million people (mostly impoverished or landless peasants) had emigrated, the majority of them to overseas destinations, especially to the United States. They were followed by the over two million migrants or displaced persons who left Polish lands during the First World War, then by nearly two million more who emigrated in the years 1918-1939 and, finally, by more than 5 million who crossed the borders during the Second World War (e.g. Kersten, 1974; Pilch and Zgorniak, 1984).

The history of Polish mass outbound migrations may be divided into five periods: (1) from the late 19th century to 1939 (during that period, migrations were, for the most part, economically motivated); (2) 1939-1944: years characterised by forced population displacements, closely related to wartime developments; (3) 1944-1980: in this period, the most important developments in terms of movement of people were the repatriation of Poles from the USSR, the migration of ethnic Germans from Poland under intergovernmental agreements, and emigration by people of Jewish origin; (4) the migrations of the 1980s; and (5) the transition period (the 1990s).

During the entire post-war period, migration waves from Poland either intensified or abated depending on the socio-political situation in the country. Between 1945 and 1989, all legislation on foreign migration reflected isolationist principles: they were simply repressive.

Till the end of the Second World War, Polish migration may be typified by looking at the two basic types of international migrants, the emigrant/immigrant and the re-migrant, as distinguished on the basis of migrant's relation to the sending area, receiving area, main impetus for migration and the duration of his or her migration. After the war, apart from the pre-existing types, another type of international migrant, very characteristic of the Polish political and economic reality, appeared: the shuttle (pendular) migrant. The quantitative and qualitative analysis of emigration from Poland by type of migrant is developed in some sections of this chapter.

Table 2.1 Three types of international migrants

Types of migrants	Relation to region of departure	Relation to region of arrival	Main impulse for change of region	Time horizon of migration
Emigrant/ Immigrant	Roots, descent, departure, farewell	Integration, new homeland	Economic, Socio-cultural Political	Long-term Unlimited
Re-migrant	Continuous point of life reference	Maintain difference, 'host country'	Economic Political	Limited
Shuttle (Circular) Migrant	Defined as place of permanent life	Defined as place of working or possibility of quick enrichment	Economic	Very short- or short time Limited

Source: Author's concept on the basis of Pries (1999)

Following A. Pilch and M. Zgorniak (Pilch and Zgorniak, 1984), post-war emigration may be classified as:

- Direct emigration (leaving Poland for temporary or permanent residence abroad);
- Indirect emigration, which involved primarily soldiers, prisoners of war and ethnic minority groups, in other words everybody unable to

return to Poland after the Second World War who emigrated to other countries from the places they found themselves at the time.

This chapter is concerned with direct post-war migrations. The scale and pace of that process were determined by several factors of political, social and economic natures. This analysis of migration will break the post-war migration period into the sub-periods of: (i) 1945-1960, (ii) 1960-1980, (iii) the migrations of the 1980s and (iv) migrations during the transition period (the 1990s).[1]

In the post war period, Western European countries' liberal policy towards immigrant workers (especially till the 1973 crisis) did not influence migration from communist Poland. It was, let me reiterate, mainly the Polish state's restrictive passport and exit-visa policy that shaped outflows from Poland. In the official Polish policy, the concept of a "declared change of permanent residence" was (and still is) a basic concept used in defining outflows and, likewise, inflows.[2] Therefore, due to fear of repression, those who wanted to spend years abroad in order to earn money did not declare it officially during the communist era. Some of them, and especially those who were given the stark option of "you may leave, but it will be forever" settled abroad, fewer risked persecution and returned home after a prolonged stay abroad.

The liberalisation of Polish state policy after 1989 coincided with the imposition of direct or indirect restrictions on foreign workers or on migration based on ethnic claims in northwestern European countries. This meant that getting a job or obtaining *Aussiedlers* status in Germany stopped being so easy for Poles in the 1990s. The more restrictive immigration policy of some northwestern European countries was one of the factors behind the decrease of "illegal" (unregistered) outflow from Poland and changes in the destination countries in the case of income-generating migration. Therefore, in the transition period it was again state policy that affected outflows from Poland, with the difference that it was not Polish regulations but the immigration policy of Western European countries that was at play. This thesis will be elaborated throughout this chapter.

Knowledge about migration from Poland after the Second World War is insufficient and the official statistical registries are deficient. The deficiency of the official data is obvious when comparing Polish statistics on emigration and receiving countries' data on immigration. Serious under recordings occur in Polish sources. For example, certain kinds of emigration to Germany in the 1980s (of ethnic Germans, their family members and those who simply took advantage of the loose policy of the Federal Republic of Germany to get *Aussiedler* status) was not registered for the most part. Between 1980 and 1989, according to the official statistics, around 271,000 people emigrated whereas the estimated number (Okolski, 1994) for this period was 1.1-1.3 million (the majority of them to Germany). German sources put the number at between 700,000 and 800,000 people.

While analysing Poles' international migrations in the 1990s, one must also bear in mind that, as of 1989, virtually no data on individual departures (formerly collected by the SERP passport traffic registration system) have been gathered. Nor are any other records kept of foreign travel by Poles.

Since, however, the official data turn out to be the only source that make an analysis of the general trends and structure of migration over the whole post-war period possible, this author has decided to base some part of the following sections on this source. However, as already mentioned, official statistics concerning changes of the permanent residence address in connection with moving abroad are incomplete and should only be analysed with caution.

Years 1945-1960

The wartime resettlements of 1939-1944 were the decisive factor that would later determine the movements of people in the first 15 post-war years, from 1945 to 1960. While it has been claimed that the migrations of that era were a general consequence of the post-war political and territorial changes in the country, the war itself was, in fact, the prime cause of all the post-war changes. In the 1945-1960 period, three characteristic sub-periods may be distinguished in terms of migration: (i) 1945-1950 (ii) 1951-1955 and (iii) 1956-1960.

(i) 1945-1950: during this period, populations of non-Polish ancestry were moved and resettled from Polish territory under international agreements. These were the Potsdam Agreement (Potsdam, August 1945), the Polish-Soviet agreement (August 1945) and the Polish-Czechoslovak treaty (March 1947). These agreements were closely related to the reformation of the Polish state within its newly delineated borders. Some 6.5 million people resettled or were resettled out of and into Poland during the six years immediately following the war (Pilch, 1994). Germany, the USSR and Israel were the main directions of emigration from Poland at that time.

Germany-bound: as early as August 1945, approximately half a million Germans left Poland, either fleeing or in unorganised resettlements. Between February 1946 and April 1950, an organised resettlement operation was carried out, which resulted in about 2.3 million Germans leaving Poland. In 1946-1947, women with children and the elderly accounted for the vast majority of departures (approximately 2.2 million).

The remaining 100,000 people left between 1948 and 1950. These were mainly prisoners of war, qualified workers and orphans (Latuch, 1961). A total of 4,092,200 people left between 1945 and 1950: 1,121,700 in 1945; 2,225,200 in 1946; 538,500 in 1947; 42,700 in 1948; 34,100 in 1949 and 87,200 in 1950 (Latuch, 1961).

USSR-bound: in the years 1945-1946, 481,183 Ukrainians, 36,393 Belorussians and about 1,000 Lithuanians left Poland under a repatriation agreement between Poland and the USSR (Latuch, 1961). The repatriation was completed in August 1946.

Israel-bound: in the "option for Israel" period (from 13 September, 1949, to 31 December, 1950), over 38,000 applications for emigration were considered (not counting children under the age of 13), about 1/3 of which were turned down. The foreign sources on emigration to Israel that claim that 120,000 Jews left Poland for Israel between 1945 and 1950 are mistaken and the figures they provide must not be considered as reliable. According to some Polish estimates (Latuch, 1961), there were no more than 60,000 persons of Jewish origin left in Poland after World War II. The misguided West European statistics rely on the category of "place of birth," this is misleading as it refers to the number of Polish-born Jews who resettled in Israel from various countries of the world, not from just Poland.

Other out-migration directions in the sub-period under analysis include the USA, Canada, France, Britain and Argentina. The data on these migrations are, however, fragmentary.

(ii) 1951-1955: this period saw a relative stagnation in the movement of people out of Poland as a result of outward migration being brought to a near standstill for political reasons. The movements that did exist generally occurred along one corridor, and mostly involved migrations to and from East Germany. During that period, there was also a relatively negligible emigration to Israel. Overall, the movements of people between 1951 and 1955 measured only in the tens of thousands.

(iii) 1956-1960: some 600,000 people moved into and out of Poland over that period. The migrations of that period are a continuation of the interrupted 1945-1950 movements. The entire period displays features similar to the movements of the immediate post-war years. It is characterised, basically, by mass repatriation from the USSR to Poland and by emigration to Germany under the 'family reunion' scheme. The migrations headed to some 30 countries in a hierarchical order similar to that characteristic of the 1945-1950 period.

Germany-bound: the Potsdam resettlements involving over three million ethnic Germans had been completed by 1950. According to Polish Red Cross estimates, about 160,000 Germans remained in Poland after 1951. Further migrations to take up permanent residence in either of the two German states occurred either under direct agreements between the East German and Polish state authorities,[3] or through the Polish and West German Red Cross organisations.[4] Between 1952 and 1955, 10,800 people emigrated to East Germany and 737 people to West Germany.

In December 1955, the Central Committee of the Polish United Workers' Party (KC PZPR) passed a resolution obligating the Ministry of the Interior to take a more favourable approach while considering ethnic Germans' applications to emigrate, and to grant emigration permits to individuals unfit for work, women, children and pensioners seeking to reunite with their families. In April 1957, the Secretariat of the KC PZPR passed a resolution that extended the emigration criteria to cover all ethnic Germans, regardless of whether they held Polish citizenship (Lempinski, 1987).

The two aforementioned resolutions turned emigration to Germany into a mass phenomenon as early as 1957, reaching a scale that took both the Polish and the West German Red Cross organisations by surprise (Lempinski, 1987). 253,130 people left Poland between 1956 and February 1959, of whom 216,062 left for West Germany and 37,068 for East Germany. Such a scale of emigration from Poland to both German states, and in particular to West Germany, resulted from the intensifying migration by members of the indigenous Polish populations of the "Regained Territories," as the formerly German northern and western territories were termed. The "family reunion" scheme provided these people with another opportunity to choose their nationality.

Research into the family reunion scheme has shown that the interpretation of the official emigration criteria was by no means unequivocal, as emigration permits were even granted to full families of Polish nationality and citizenship.[5] Upon crossing the border, they forfeited their Polish citizenship.

In the period under consideration, the emigration policy of the Polish state was characterised by two factors: (a) an improvement of settlement conditions for Polish repatriates from the USSR and (b) a misconceived plan for the "elimination of hostile and temporary elements." The authorities of the Polish People's Republic (PRL) sought to create an ethnically homogenous state. To quote Latuch (1961, p. 39), "One may venture an opinion that, had it not been for the repatriation of ethnic Poles from the USSR, emigration to Germany would never have reached its actual scale."

Israel-bound: migrations to Israel had the particular character of emigration in the strict sense of the term. It was, for the most part, emigration by whole families.[6] Between 1955 and 1960, 51,137 people emigrated to Israel.

Table 2.2 Emigration to Israel, 1955-1960

Years	Persons (absolute numbers)
1955	192
1956	9384
1957	30331
1958	3143
1959	3561
1960	4526

Source: Latuch, 1961, p. 53

The increase in emigration to Israel is attributable, to a certain degree, to emigration by repatriates of Jewish descent who had returned from the USSR. Their return coincided with a difficult and complicated political and economic situation. They came into direct contact with a Jewish community in Poland that was overcome by an emigration psychosis due, among other things, to mounting nationalism and anti-Semitism. Emigration to Israel involved especially people who had been settled on the northern and western territories. In 1956, out of a total of 22,000 applications for emigration, 60 per cent were from the Wroclaw voivodship (province). In 1957, 57 per cent of applications were from the same voivodship.

Table 2.3 Emigration from Poland by main countries of destination, 1955-1960

Country	1955	1956	1957	1958	1959	1960
Great Britain	47	177	414	524	391	432
France	44	122	333	611	383	399
East Germany (DDR)	413	5606	23637	1500	2141	1068
West Germany (FRG)	737	14945	90317	106589	10087	6628
Israel	192	9384	30331	3143	3561	4526
Argentina	–	–	–	164	123	94
Brazil	–	–	–	161	118	163
Canada	83	236	605	2762	2943	2606
USA	72	261	911	2254	3950	6058
Australia	–	–	–	–	1528	1433
Total	2325	33036	148472	1457	29774	24050

Source: Latuch, 1961, p. 55

Other destinations: since 1958, an increase in emigration headed to countries other than Germany and Israel may be observed. In particular, migrations to the USA, Canada and Australia intensified to the extent that total emigration to these three countries outnumbered emigration to both German states in 1960. Other major destinations were Britain and France.

Years 1960-1980

Between 1960 and 1970, permanent emigration stabilised at a level of about 22,000 emigrants annually; 1965 was the only year when that level was significantly exceeded (Wasilewska-Trenkner, 1973). Temporary emigration to what was then termed "capitalist countries" grew steadily between 1956 and 1960 following the 1951-1955 interruption. Other types of migrations exhibited a similar trend. An analysis of the dynamics of permanent emigration volumes by country of destination shows a distinct dominance of resettlements in two areas: the two German states and North America (see Table 2.4). Between 1960 and 1970, these two destinations absorbed 78.5 per cent of the overall number of permanent emigrants, i.e. some 200,000 people (approximately 131,000 to West and East Germany, and about 62,000 to the USA and Canada).

The dynamics of migratory directions display characteristic patterns. While migrations to the two Germanys and Israel fluctuated greatly, in migrations to the USA and Canada a steady increase may be observed between 1960 and 1965, followed by a marked fall in the latter half of the decade. The decrease in emigration in the mid- to late-60s was probably related to the introduction of stricter immigration policies by the receiving countries at that time. Migrations to take up permanent residence in Britain or France displayed a distinct downward trend.

While 89.6 per cent of permanent emigrants were bound for the destinations named in Table 2.4, the states in question received only a negligible percentage of temporary emigrants (Wasilewska-Trenkner, 1973).

According to Wasilewska-Trenkner's (1973) estimates, between 1960 and 1970, 25.2 per cent of temporary emigrants migrated to either of the German states, 6.8 per cent to France and Britain, and a mere 1.7 per cent to Canada and the USA. The other destinations of temporary emigrants were Austria, Italy and Scandinavia.

The question of permanent emigration is extremely interesting as analysed from the point of view of Poland's territorial structure. Between 1966 and 1970, residents of the Katowice (28.4 per cent of all permanent emigrants), Olsztyn (12 per cent) and Opole (13.5 per cent) voivodships

Table 2.4 Emigration from Poland by main countries of destination, 1960-1970

Years	Total	Germany (East and West)	Israel	Canada and USA	Great Britain and France
1960	24050	7696	4526	8663	831
1961	22397	10040	744	8256	589
1962	20789	10161	666	7283	590
1963	20076	7701	476	9356	714
1964	25373	13122	877	8452	778
1965	32113	17457	911	10525	795
1966	28755	20459	538	5677	527
1967	21857	15592	406	4016	458
1968	17201	10395	3437	1946	321
1969	22473	11047	7674	2172	368
1970	10310	6527	698	4174	327
Total	245394	130197	20953	62264	6380
Percentage of emigration in a given destination	100	53.1	8.5	25.4	2.6

Source: Wasilewska-Trenkner, 1973, p. 42

(provinces) were the most likely to leave Poland to take up permanent residence abroad (see Table 2.5). The Lublin (1 per cent), Kielce (1.3 per cent) and Koszalin (1.5 per cent) voivodships were the ones to contribute the fewest migrants. As regards overseas emigration (the USA, Canada, Australia), the greatest numbers of permanent migrants came form the Bialystok, Krakow, Rzeszow and Wroclaw voivodships. Emigrants to either German state came almost exclusively from the Katowice, Olsztyn and Opole voivodships. The most intensive emigration to Britain and France was from the Katowice, Warsaw and Wroclaw voivodships, while emigrants to Israel were mostly residents of the Lodz, Warsaw and Wroclaw voivodships.

Overseas emigration from Poland to the USA and Canada diminished in the 1970s. According to American and Canadian estimates, in the three decades between 1950 and 1980, the numbers of emigrants from Poland in these countries were as follows (see Table 2.6). The juxtaposed values show that migrations to the USA and Canada fell by over 30 per cent in the 1970s as compared to the 1960-1970 period (31 per cent and 33 per cent, respectively).

Table 2.5 Emigration from Poland by sending areas and destination country, 1966-1970 (%)

Sending areas (voivod-ships)	Total	Great Britain	Australia	CSRR	France	Israel	Canada	FRG	DDR	USA	USRR
Total	100.0	100.0	100.0	100.0	100.0	100.0	100.0	100.0	100.0	100.0	100.0
Bialystok	3.1	2.4	4.3	0.5	1.4	0.7	3.6	0.2	0.3	12.1	9.2
Bydgoszcz	1.6	4.9	3.1	0.8	1.3	0.6	2.7	0.2	0.7	3.3	0.5
Gdansk	2.3	9.4	7.5	1.0	2.1	1.0	4.4	1.0	2.2	2.8	3.3
Katowice	28.4	12.1	7.1	34.9	13.7	9.3	4.8	48.3	39.7	3.2	6.8
Kielce	1.3	1.2	4.4	1.1	2.2	0.3	5.1	0.0	0.2	3.0	0.8
Koszalin	1.5	3.8	2.6	0.4	1.1	0.1	2.8	0.5	1.3	1.7	5.0
Krakow	4.8	8.6	9.8	31.2	7.8	2.7	8.2	0.1	0.2	18.6	1.5
Lublin	1.0	2.7	5.0	0.6	2.0	0.9	7.3	0.0	0.1	3.6	4.9
Lodz	3.0	3.8	8.5	2.2	5.3	10.4	3.7	0.7	1.5	2.5	2.3
Olsztyn	12.0	4.5	3.9	1.2	0.3	0.1	4.0	23.6	23.1	4.0	8.8
Opole	13.5	2.1	2.4	5.7	2.2	0.5	3.5	22.3	19.8	1.6	6.7
Poznan	1.8	4.4	3.0	1.5	4.3	0.4	2.7	0.4	1.0	1.9	2.2
Rzeszow	5.4	3.8	5.8	1.8	7.0	0.6	13.0	0.0	0.1	18.7	3.4
Szczecin	2.3	4.3	4.6	1.1	3.6	6.8	5.2	0.6	1.4	2.8	7.2
Warsaw	6.4	16.8	9.4	2.2	6.0	33.4	8.2	0.1	0.3	10.3	5.1
Wroclaw	9.4	12.1	15.4	11.1	37.2	30.7	15.1	1.6	5.6	7.3	25.7
Zielona-Gora	2.3	2.8	3.2	2.7	2.5	1.5	5.7	0.4	2.7	2.6	6.6

Source: Wasilewska-Trenkner, 1973, p. 49

Table 2.6 Emigrants from Poland in USA and Canada, 1950-1980

Years	Countries	
	USA (a)	Canada (a)
1951-1960	9985	2703
1961-1970	53539	15215
1971-1980	37234	10256
Total	100758	28174

(a) by country of birth

Source: Slany, 1991, p. 38

The *Notification by the Government of the Polish People's Republic* (PRL) announced on 18 November, 1970, was the direct cause for a dramatic increase in the number of applicants for permanent emigration to West Germany.[7] As of 31 December, 1971, 131,823 such applications had been filed, an increase of more than 54,000 over 1970. At the same time, German statistics put the number of persons eligible for migration from Poland, both on grounds of family reunion and of self-affiliation with the German people, at 270,000. Up to 1975, the emigrants who had actually migrated pursuant to applications filed under the Notification criteria made up a relatively small percentage of all applicants for emigration.[8] Between 1970 and 1975, 62,484 people immigrated in West Germany. The migrants' territorial origin pattern in that period continued unchanged from the 1960s. Thus, migration from the "Regained Territories," including a high percentage of indigenous Poles, prevailed (Lempinski, 1987). There were 16,250 people who migrated from the Opole voivodship, which accounted for 26 per cent of total emigration from Poland to West Germany, 15,500 from the Katowice voivodship (24.8 per cent), and 6,250 from the Olsztyn voivodship (10 per cent).

After mid-1976, matters of emigration to the Federal Republic of Germany were governed by the "Protocol Provision" of 7 October, 1975.[9] The provision specified that between 120,000 and 125,000 people met the emigration criteria, and that their applications were to be granted within four years, i.e. between 1976 and 1979.[10] The figure completely disagreed with the West German assumptions, made prior to the Helsinki negotiations, when the German Red Cross (GRC) determined that the number of individuals meeting the emigration criteria was 283,000. However, soon after the provision became effective, an "open clause" was added to it that abolished the time limit for granting applications.

The Protocol Provision, together with the open clause, established a legal status that was clearly related to one-way movement of people from Poland to West Germany. As interpreted by the German side, the negotiated arrangement covered those Polish citizens who were regarded in the Federal Republic of Germany as having ties to both the German state and the German nation. As interpreted by the Polish side, given the fact that neither the institution of dual citizenship nor, more importantly, "self-affiliation with the German people," were recognised under Polish legislation, the stipulations of the provision meant applicants were forced to renounce their Polish heritage and citizenship prior to migration. As a result, migrations by stateless persons occurred, who were bound for their supposed homeland as "repatriates."

In the 1970s, the prevalence of ethnic Poles among the migrants became obvious. Articles in emigration regulations forced migrating ethnic

Poles to give up their Polish nationality while still on the territory of the Polish state. In this case, their disavowal had a formal and legal character resulting in the loss of their Polish citizenship.[11] Within the first four years of the implementation of the provision, i.e. between 30 June, 1976, and 30 June, 1980, a total of 122,725 people migrated to the Federal Republic of Germany.

In the late 1970s, another form of emigration became increasingly common, with Polish citizens who had arrived to stay temporarily ultimately taking up permanent residence in West Germany. Between 1976 and 1979, 20,158 people took up permanent residence in West Germany in this way, and another 3,485 people by 30 June 1980 (i.e. when the provision went out of effect). Overall, during the implementation of the provision, 152,887 people permanently left Polish territory, including 122,725 legally, under emigration permits issued by the Polish authorities.

The emigrants' provincial origin pattern did not change significantly. The trend towards emigration to Germany strengthened dramatically in the Katowice voivodship: 58,607 people migrated from this voivodship between 1976 and 1979 (which accounted for nearly 44 per cent of all emigrants from Poland to West Germany). Emigration from the Opole voivodship totalled 39,420 people (29.6 per cent), and from the Olsztyn voivodship 20,158 people (15.1 per cent).

Emigration During the 1980s

Cross-border migrations by Poles, which assumed a mass scale precisely during that period, were an extremely grave consequence of the social, political and economic crisis that hit Poland in the 1980s.

While economically-motivated migrations prevailed, political emigration intensified in the early 1980s as a result of the 1981 imposition of martial law and the repercussions in its aftermath. The USA, Canada and Australia continued being the major destinations for overseas immigration. Among outflows bound for overseas, family and refugee migrations prevailed.

Compared to inflows from other regions of the world, emigration from Poland made up only a small proportion of the total influx into the three aforementioned countries between 1980 and 1989, accounting for 1.3 per cent, 4.3 per cent and 1.5 per cent, respectively.[12] The official American, Canadian and Australian statistics indicate that 22,485 people emigrated from Poland to Australia, 68,792 people (by the last country of permanent residence) or 76,818 people (by the country of birth) to the USA and

38,642 to Australia between 1980 and 1989. From the statistics on emigration from Poland for the preceding decades (see Table 2.6), it is evident that the number of USA immigrants from Poland nearly doubled in the 1980s over the previous decade, while the number of Poles in Canada increased four times over the same period.

If such considerations of migration as very long distances, greater potential risks involved in an overseas as compared to continental migration, high travel costs, etc., are taken into account, it may be concluded that the inflow from Poland is sizeable, which is of great consequence for the country of origin as well (Slany, 1991).

Other available figures (foreign statistics) on migrations by Poles in the 1980s indicate that 18,393 people emigrated to Austria, 3,360 to the UK, 5,700 to France, 22,000 to Switzerland, 1,200 to Norway and 16,800 to Sweden over the period under consideration. These figures cover exclusively those who sought to legalise their residence abroad (registering with Norway's Central Population Register; granted one-year work permits in Switzerland and Sweden; or remaining under the control of the International Migration Office in Austria, the UK and France) (Slany, 1991). The aforementioned official registers certainly underestimate the actual migration figures and should therefore be analysed with considerable caution.

According to a Governmental Population Commission (GPC) estimate, some 670,000 people left Poland to take up temporary residence abroad, some 96,000 to take up permanent residence abroad, and 66,000 went abroad on business, military or other professional duty between 1981 and 1988.

Thus, according to the GPC, the migrations of the 1980s involved 830,000 people (GPC, 1989). The most recent estimates of the scale of emigration between 1980 and 1989, based on the data obtained from the Central Population Register (PESEL) system and the Passport Traffic Registration (SERP) sub-system, Central Statistical Office figures, Western statistics and other available sources on migration (such as employment agencies) indicate that the total number of emigrants in the 1980s decade was somewhere between 2,205,000 and 2,345,000 (Okolski, 1994).

Relying on the same estimates, the number of long-term migrants (i.e. those who had spent over 12 months abroad) has been put at 1,073,000-1,317,000. By subtracting the total number of long-term emigrants from the total number of people who migrated abroad, we can easily calculate the number of short-term emigrants over that period, which comes to between 1,028,000 and 1,132,000. The result shows that in the 1980s long-term emigration was more common than short-term emigration, as was the case, indeed, over the whole 1945-1989 period (Okolski, 1994). Most temporary migrants went to West Germany (about 45 per cent of the total number of emigrants), the USA (about 14 per cent), Italy and Austria. The two latter countries were not final destinations but, rather, a stop on the way to overseas destinations, that is to say the USA, Canada and Australia. Approximately 80 per cent of all permanent emigrants went to West Germany.

Half of the approximately 830,000 people who left the country between 1981 and 1988 came from only five of the forty-nine voivodships Poland then had: the Katowice, Opole, Warsaw, Gdansk and Wroclaw voivodships.[13] Notwithstanding an unusually high proportion of women among the emigrants noted by the official statistics from 1981 to 1988 (159 women per 100 men), according to more reliable estimates the proportions between the sexes were almost equal (women slightly prevailed). This may suggest that, in many cases, unofficial male emigration preceded official female emigration (by wives, often with children). Almost twice as many women declared a desire to emigrate permanently.

The migrations of the 1980s were decidedly selective from the point of view of demographic and social characteristics. It was the young, working-age, skilled, professionally-mobile and active people who migrated. Between 1980 and 1989, the flow of people out of the country (the long-term emigration stream) was so great that it outnumbered the natural increase in 1988-1989 (Okolski, 1994).

At this point, I will discuss at some length migrations to Germany in the 1980s in view of the mass character of the phenomenon, whose consequences, I believe, are to be expected for decades to come.

Since the early 1980s, emigration from Poland to West Germany was governed by the so-called "open clause" agreed in connection with the Protocol Provision. This meant, for individuals meeting the emigration criteria set down in the *Notification by the Government of the Polish People's Republic*, that the Polish authorities granted permits for emigration to West Germany even after the expiry of the 4-year period fixed in the provision. However, persons to whom the clause applied made up only some 40 per cent of all those who moved permanently to West Germany over that period. The reason is that, in the period under analysis, illegal emigration was most common.

Illegal migrations assumed mass proportions especially in 1984-1985, when this type of migration accounted for over 80 per cent of overall migration to Germany. Between 1980 and 1985, 166,630 people emigrated from Poland to West Germany (see Table 2.7).

The growing illegal emigration was due mostly to the way that Poland's internal situation evolved. Not only did illegal migrations increase

Table 2.7 Emigration from Poland to Germany, 1980-1985

Years	Legal (registered) emigration		Illegal (unregistered) emigration		Total
	Absolute numbers	%	Absolute numbers	%	
1980	17157	64.4	9480	35.6	26637
1981	23489	46.1	27494	53.9	50983
1982	15550	51.2	14807	48.8	30357
1983	10993	57.5	8128	42.5	19121
1984	3073	17.6	14384	82.4	17457
1985	2571	11.6	19504	88.4	22075
Total	72833	–	93797	–	166630

Source: Lempiski, 1987, p. 89

the scale of the problem of reuniting families, but they also expanded the scope of emigration from Poland to West Germany in terms of the emigrants' territorial origin. From 1980 to 1985, there were over 85,000 emigrants from the Katowice voivodship, accounting for 51.2 per cent of all (legal and illegal) permanent migrations from Poland to West Germany. The trend was also related to growing emigration among the indigenous, ethnically Polish population of the part of Upper Silesia that had belonged to Poland prior to the Second World War (the "old territories"). As this population was strongly integrated through family ties with Polish communities from Poland's other regions, permanent migrations to West Germany by indigenous inhabitants of the old territories of Upper Silesia opened certain opportunities for the drainage of people residing outside the traditional regions of migration to Germany, i.e. the Katowice, Olsztyn and Opole voivodships.

The growing rate of emigration from Poland to West Germany in the 1980s indicates that a new demographic pool had emerged that was acquiring migration entitlements. Its arising is attributable both to people from different areas headed to West Germany and to the occurrence of new cases of family reunions as a result of illegal emigration.

In the 1980s, migrations became a popular reaction to the social and economic crisis and a way to avoid or escape its consequences. The number of Polish citizens remaining either illegally or in contravention of Polish regulations in the West, which often involved seeking asylum or immigrant status, manifested this.

Seasonal economic migration, developing between Poland and what was then termed "capitalist countries," was another form in which migration trends were manifested throughout the country. It is impossible, however, to present this type of emigration in numerical terms.

Emigration During the Transition Period (1990s)

The gradual liberalisation of Poland's passport policy (initiated in 1985) culminated in the free availability of passports and, consequently, freedom of foreign travel for all citizens, granted by the last communist cabinet in 1988. The regulation took effect in 1989. That very year, the first non-communist Polish cabinet declared its highly liberal stance on foreign travel. Citizens' rights to freely leave their place of residence, to travel abroad and even to settle in a foreign country were recognised. Many of the restrictions on foreigners' entry into Poland were lifted (Okolski, 1994). In August 1991, the Polish government ratified the 1951 Geneva Convention and the New York Protocol on Refugees. By the end of 1994, visa-free regime agreements had been signed with 45 countries. Furthermore, Poland had signed a number of international agreements on academic exchange programmes involving college and university teachers and students. A package of bilateral agreements on the employment of Polish workers in certain West European countries, in particular in West Germany, was an extra factor stimulating migrations in the early 1990s (Okolski, 1994).

By analysing permanent outflows by five-year annual averages (see Figure 2.1), we can see that emigration since 1989 reached its lowest level since 1960 (with the exception of years 1970-1974). Emigration from Poland during the transition period was about 40 per cent below the average of 29,800 for 1985-1989 and about 19 per cent lower than the average of 24,400 for 1980-1984. There were many factors conducive to the decline of this outflow.

It is this author's opinion that the greatest contributing factor to the drop was the new developments, challenges and opportunities presented to a quite large part of the society (especially the cohort of younger urban professionals) by the political, social and economic transformation and the market-based revaluation of the zloty. However, the transformation also brought on economic hardship for some. Some segments of society (especially the working class rural dwellers, the middle-aged and the poorly educated) faced such negative phenomena as unemployment, difficulties with adaptation to the market requirements and financial or job insecurity. All this affected migration patterns following the collapse of the old system. To support this thesis, trends in emigration by such migrants' features as: sex, age, place of residence, education and destination country are analysed below.

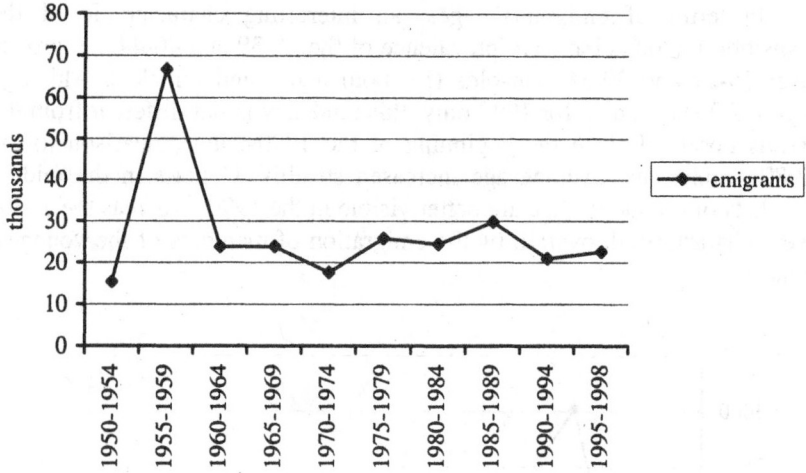

Source: Central Statistical Office

Figure 2.1 Emigration from Poland, 1950-1998

After many years of females outnumbering males, in 1994 the number of males topped (by 8 per cent) the number of females. This tendency was kept up in the second half of the 1990s, meaning that a pattern, characteristic of the communist era, whereby men would migrate illegally and be followed by legal female migration had been broken. The reversal of females' domination in official statistics also indicates that the unregistered ("illegal") outflow from Poland must have declined during the transition period.

Table 2.8 Emigrants by sex, 1981-1998

Year	Total	Males	Females
1981-1985	120148	54686	65462
1986-1990	146820	68668	78152
1991-1995	112716	56686	56039
1995	26344	13305	13039
1996	21297	10882	10415
1997	20222	10179	10043
1998	22177	11607	10570

Source: Rocznik Demograficzny (Demographic Yearbook), Central Statistical Office, GUS, (CSO) Warsaw, 1998, p. 340

In terms of emigrants' ages, an interesting characteristic of the transition period is the clear prevalence of the 35-39 and 40-44 age groups over 25-29 and 30-34 year-olds (for both males and females). Although figure 2.2 shows data for 1997 only, this tendency is not different from the trends observed since the beginning of the 1990s; in comparison to the 1980s, emigrants' average age increased steadily. Cohorts in the middle brackets of productive age are better visible in the 1990s whereas the 1980s were characterised, overall, by the emigration of members of the youngest cohorts.

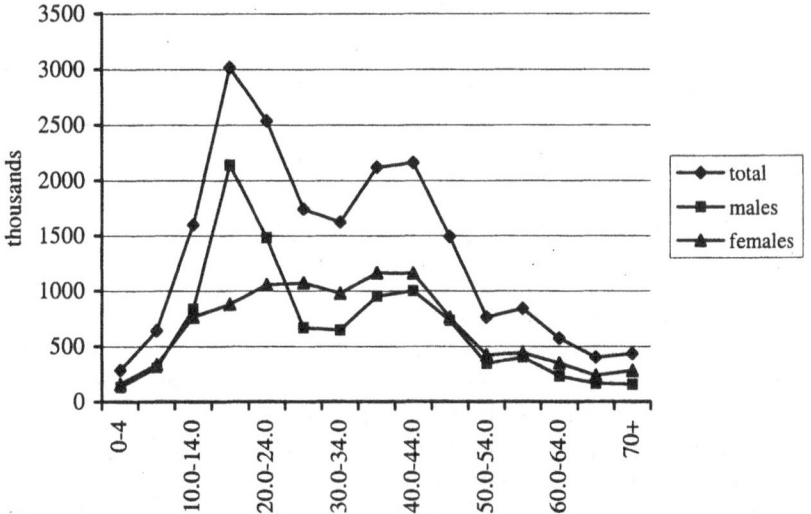

Source: Central Statistical Office

Figure 2.2 Emigration by age and sex in 1997

One can see from Figure 2.3 that among the emigrants, young inhabitants of urban areas dominate significantly. A highly uneven geographic distribution of outflows, which was visible in the 1980s, kept up in the 1990s. About 50 per cent of migrants left from four of the most urban and industrialised areas: Warsaw, Gdansk, Katowice and Opole.

The lowly educated were dominant among Polish migrants; furthermore their proportion was consistently on the rise through the 1990s. However, there was no indication of a brain drain, as existed at the beginning of the 1980s. The surge of academics among emigrants during the periods of Solidarity and martial law was very significant.

Patterns of Emigration 31

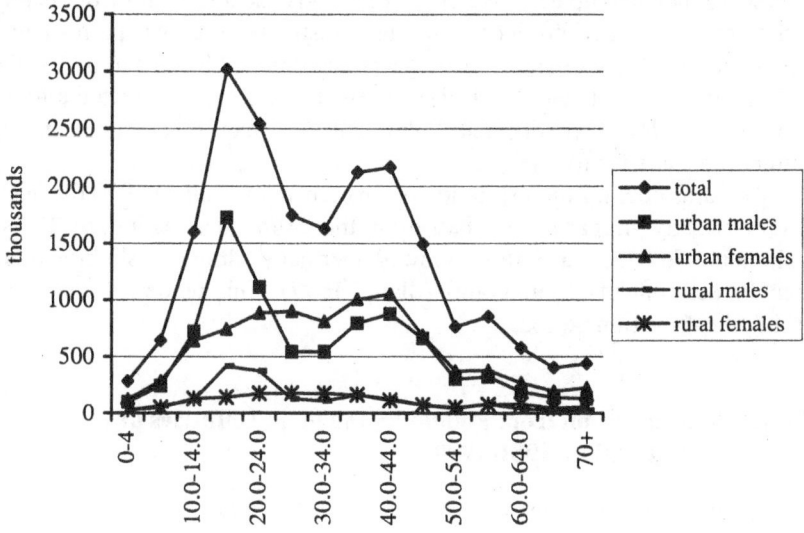

Source: Central Statistical Office

Figure 2.3 Emigration by age, sex and place of residence in 1997

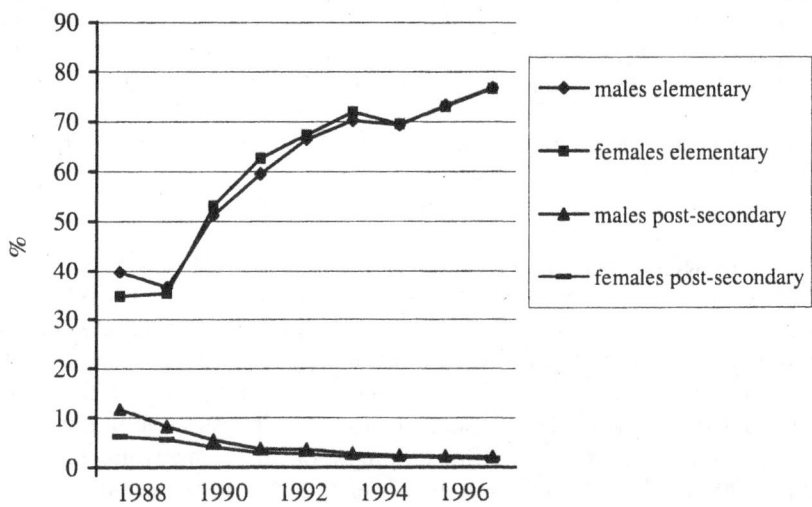

Source: Okolski, 1998c, p. 19

Figure 2.4 Emigrants (15+) by two extreme educational categories (%)

This wave included up to 15 per cent of all Polish scholars, most frequently computer scientists, physicists and biologists, who either permanently emigrated or left the country on long-term contracts, bound mainly for the United States (Hryniewicz et al., 1992). The transformation created a lot of opportunities for well-educated Poles and this fact is mirrored in the emigration statistics for the 1990s.

As far as country of destination is concerned, ever since 1950 the West (and Germany in particular) has been the prime destination of Polish emigrants. The United States followed Germany, drawing slightly more than 10 per cent of all emigrants (Slany, 1997). This tendency continued during the transition period.

Table 2.9 Emigration from Poland by the main countries of destination, 1981-1998

Country of destination	1981-1985	1986-1990	1991-1995	1995	1996	1997	1998
Europe total	99007	120733	90497	20917	17005	16289	18446
Germany	73362	87631	79667	18105	14800	14187	16128
France	4230	4962	1482	368	255	243	266
Sweden	3787	3916	2119	578	365	283	250
USA	11924	14654	12656	3179	2490	2223	2217
Canada	4273	6987	7291	1682	1348	990	1076
Total	120148	146820	112725	26277	21297	20210	22177

Source: Rocznik Statystyczny (Statistical Yearbook), Central Statistical Office, GUS, Warsaw, 1995, p. 70

What seems to be the most important finding from the analysis of these fragmentary statistics covering exclusively the registered outflow is the fact that the political factor did not play an important role in changes in population mobility from Poland. The collapse of the system and the liberalisation of migration policy did not cause massive emigration from Poland. Nor did the Federal Republic of Germany's restrictive immigration policy reduce the official outflow. Emigration to Germany in the years 1991-1994 totalled 73,149 persons, lower than the peak period of 1986-1989 but similar to the years 1981-1985 (see Table 2.9). However, German registers show that the number of Poles applying for *Aussiedler* status (who had been, *de facto*, a major group of Polish citizens emigrating to Germany) dropped dramatically in the 1990s (see Table 2.10).

Table 2.10 Emigration of ethnic German *Aussiedler*, central and eastern Europe and the Soviet Union, 1950-1994 (in thousand)

Country	1950-1965	1966-1980	1981-1986	1987-1990	1991-1993	1994
Czechoslovakia (a)	31	59	7	6	2	–
Poland	357	275	167	573	63	3
Romania	15	92	85	161	54	7
Soviet Union	19	67	10	308	550	213
Other	130	23	5	7	2	–
Total	552	516	274	1055	671	223
Annual average	35	34	46	264	224	223

(a) 'Former' or 'successor states', as appropriate

Source: German Statistical Office; direct communications to UN/ECE secretariat

Looking at the future of Polish migration, it seems that three factors will play important roles. These are as follows: the economic factor, the "Germany" factor and a demographic factor.

It is evident that the registered outflow declined in the 1990s mainly due to the social and economic changes and new opportunities enjoyed by what had been one of the most mobile parts of society, young and very young urban professionals. It seems that the phenomenon of emigration slowly became the domain of blue-collar workers unable to adapt to free market conditions. Assuming a moderately optimistic growth scenario for the Polish economy, in 10-15 years the wage and price disparity between Poland and the rest of the European Union is likely to have diminished to some extent. This would make segments of the society so prone for migration today become less anxious to do so and consequently reduce the potential of migration.

Since emigration to Germany at one time reached exodus proportions, the phenomenon of further emigration on the basis of either ethnic claims or family reunification will undoubtedly remain visible in future outflows. Its size is not easy to predict and the economic factor will play a very important role in determining its size. The influence of economics on shaping ethnic self-identification has been visible in Poland for long time; in recent years, interest in belonging to German minority organisations in Poland has been declining. Another phenomenon is a return to Poland of thousands of people who once claimed German identity (Heffner, 1999). These return migrants include both representatives of the native population of Silesia (with its considerable German minority) as well as those of other ethno-geographic origins, who once claimed to be German in anticipation of being better off materially in West Germany (Kurcz, 2000).

As far as a demographic factor is concerned, the vocationally-active population of Poland, i.e. 15-64 year-olds, will increase by about 960,000 people in the years 1996-2020. The year 2020 will see, however, a drop of about 570,000 in the 15-44 age group, i.e. the most mobile age brackets and an increase by 1.4 million persons in the 45 and older group. This will also be conducive to a letting up of migratory pressure (Stola, forthcoming). Of course, there will still be a demand for short-term migration or irregular mobility in accordance with the "earn there (in the West) and spend here" credo. This phenomenon, along with the analyses of strategies and migratory mechanisms, is analysed in the following sections of this chapter.

Survey: General Framework and Methodology

This section is based on some findings from in-depth migration/mobility studies based on household surveys undertaken in Lithuania, Poland and Ukraine 1994-1996 and covering developments over a twenty-year span (1975-1994). The surveys and studies were co-ordinated by the Population Activities Unit (PAU) of the United Nations' Economic Commission for Europe (ECE) in Geneva. This author participated in the Polish research team located at the Institute for Social Studies of the University of Warsaw (ISS UW). The Commission for Scientific Research also financially supported the Polish component of the project.

The main purpose of the ethnosurvey project titled "Causes and Consequences of Emigration from Poland" was to grasp the essence of the change in international migration in relation to the revolutionary changes in the political system and in the social and economic conditions in Poland, underway since mid-1989. Thus, the main focus was on the mechanism of population movements and personal characteristics of migrants before and after 1990. One of the important objectives was to study migration *de facto* rather than *de jure*. Contemporary migration is increasingly a dynamic phenomenon, one that takes on various forms and undergoes rapid transformation. This is which is particularly true at times of rapid and profound social changes. For this reason, the two basic criteria usually inherent in the definition of migration, i.e. the legality (or registrability) of flow and a minimum (intended or actual) duration of residence (or official permission to stay over a certain period of time) in the destination country were not used for the purposes of the project. Instead, it was decided to deal with all kinds of international movements, irrespective of administrative status and duration of stay, with the major exception of recreational journeys.

The main method applied in this project was the *ethnosurvey*. This method was used for the first time in Central and Eastern Europe to study migration processes. According to Massey (1987, pp. 1498-522):

> An *ethnosurvey* involves the simultaneous application of ethnographic and survey methods within a single study of multiple sites. The guiding philosophy is that qualitative and quantitative procedures complement one another, and that properly used, one's weaknesses become the other's strength, yielding a body of data with greater reliability and more internal valid than is possible to achieve using either method alone.

Furthermore, it has to be emphasised that the ethnosurvey was designed to gain a detailed understanding of the processes, causes and consequences of international migration between particular countries. In the words of Massey et al. (1987, p. 13):

> ...the *ethnosurvey* is not a technique for aggregate statistical estimation... What the method does provide is a way of understanding the social processes that underlie aggregate statistics. The strength of the *ethnosurvey* is that it provides hard information so that the social process of international migration can be described to others in a cogent and convincing way.

With this basic approach, the international migration *ethnosurvey* was then adapted to the specific conditions of Central and Eastern Europe. Sampling procedures were agreed upon, migration and migrants to be covered in the project were defined and data collection instruments were developed.

Based on prior knowledge of the patterns of international migration, communes (or "*gmina*," the smallest administrative district) were selected to provide a mix of differing socio-economic characteristics (e.g. urban and rural) and presumed types of migration patterns. Communes with an appreciable level of migration were selected, precisely because the aim of the research was to gain profound knowledge about migration processes (Iglicka et al., 1996).

The four communes selected are located in two regions, *Opole Silesia* (a part of *Upper Silesia*) in the southwest, which has some population of German origin and a relatively long tradition of emigration and *Podlaskie* where the very first generation of emigration from largely traditional communities is taking place. Historically, *Opole Silesia* was a part of Prussia (Germany) from 1763 to 1945, whereas *Podlaskie* was a part of

Russia prior to 1918. In each of the regions, a rural commune (Lubniany and Perlejewo, respectively) and a municipality-commune (Namyslow and Monki, respectively) were selected. Even though they belong to two regions relatively far apart in terms of physical distance and ethnic specificity, all four communes seem to have much in common. Okolski (1998b, p. 36) points to four of them: i) almost all inhabitants in these communes are ethnic Poles and almost all are Catholics; ii) all communes under study are small; in no case does their population size exceed 20,000; iii) the character of the economy, administration, and socio-cultural life is generally provincial, and in many respects self-contained; iv) despite their provincial character, the propensity to migrate abroad in all four communes is relatively high (Iglicka 2000a).

The preferred household sampling procedure within the communes was to apply all the principles of strict random sampling. A two-phase household sampling strategy was adopted. In the first stage, a short, preliminary questionnaire was applied to all randomly selected households to identify households as migrant or non-migrant. The completion rates fell between 64 per cent (Perlejewo) and 78 per cent (Monki) and could be described as typical for random samples in social studies carried out in Poland. A household interview schedule was then applied in all migrant households. The sample sizes were: Namyslow (the Silesian urban commune) 123 households, Lubniany (the Silesian rural commune) 98 households; Monki (the Podlaskie region municipal commune) 109 households and Perlejewo (the Podlaskie region rural commune) 95 households. The interview sample of migrant households constituted 2.9 per cent of total number of households in Namyslow, 3.5 per cent in Lubniany, 3.4 per cent in Monki and 11 per cent in Perlejewo.

Survey Findings – Strategies of International Mobility

In the proceeding analysis, certain categories of migrants were established to mirror the basic knowledge and major characteristics and tendencies of the stream from Poland (see e.g. Table 2.1). As migration has been defined internationally as a change in residence lasting at least a few months, the specific definitions of migrant categories (categories 2 and 3; see Table 2.11), encompass exclusively migration of three months or longer.

Furthermore, two additional categories were introduced: the shuttle (pendular) migrant (category 1) and the settled migrant (category 4). Shuttle migrants were recognised as all migrants in the research who never (in the research period) went abroad for more than three months. In turn, settled migrants were members of a household, who were absent due to being abroad at the time of the household survey.

Table 2.11 Operational definitions of migrants types using the household survey data, 1994-1995

Migrant category	Definition
1) Shuttle (pendular)	Never traveled for longer than 3 months
	(i) Made only one trip
	(ii) Made more than one trip
2) Short-term	Traveled for at least 3 months but for less than a year
	(i) Made only one trip
	(ii) Made more than one trip
3) Long-term	Migrated at least once for at least a year
4) Settled	Was a household member prior to the trip but is no longer part of household because of settlement abroad

Source: Iglicka, 1998a, p. 58

These two categories (in contrast to the usual definitions) describe an exceptionally important phenomenon in Polish migration behaviour: i) the phenomenon of the so-called "petty traders" – people who earn money through irregular trade (or other activity) in different countries and ii) the phenomenon of settled migrants, which is very difficult to describe in the framework of the any time division for Poland because of the frequency (particularly in the 1980s) of money-earning trips lasting three, four or five years or more. It should be added that the first category (the shuttle migrant) was divided into two sub-groups: a) those who, up to the household survey date, had taken only one trip and b) those who had taken more than one trip. A similar division was applied to the second category (short-term migrants). Therefore, a total of six categories of migrants were established. Such strictly defined categories enabled us to analyse quantitative changes in each type of migration, both within a given community and also between them (Iglicka, 1998a, b; Iglicka, 2000a).

Analysis of specific migration behaviour was conducted individually for each community. The specific behaviour types were considered in the following order: settled migration, shuttle migration, short-term migration and long-term migration. The analysis of migration behaviour was made according to variables such as: year of most recent migration (in case of settled migration), year of first migration (all remaining categories), destination countries (settled and shuttle migration), number of migrations (for shuttle migration (b), short-term migration (b) and long-term migration), and the number of years spent abroad since the first migration lasting three months or longer (long-term migrations and short-term migrations (b)).

Furthermore, for each of the most important migrant categories, an analysis was conducted according to fundamental socio-demographic traits for each community.

Substantial differences in migration behaviour were noted among the four studied communities. Different types of migration dominated in each of the communes; in Lubniany the dominant type of migration behaviour was settled migration, in Namyslow – shuttle, in Perlejewo – long term, and in Monki – shuttle or settled. Therefore, it should be noted that shuttle migrants predominated in the urban communes.

Table 2.12 Predominant type of migration by commune of origin, 1994-1995 (%)

Type of migration	Lubniany	Monki	Namyslow	Perlejewo
Shuttle (pendular) of which,	27.1	29.6	67.3	17.1
– only one trip	11.9	9.4	29.8	12.5
– more than one trip	15.3	20.1	37.5	4.6
Short-term of which,	14.7	15.1	13.1	27.0
– only one trip	10.2	15.1	9.5	21.7
– more than one trip	4.5	–	3.6	5.3
Long-term	8.5	26.4	9.5	32.9
Settled	29.7	28.9	10.1	23.0
Total	100.0	100.0	100.0	100.0
Absolute numbers	177	159	168	152

Source: Iglicka, 1998a, p. 59

It should be pointed out that the migration processes begun prior to 1980 or in the early 1980s in the communes surveyed were modest. As well, almost every type of migration underwent intensification in the nineties.

Amalgamated statistics covering migration by category in the four communities show roughly the same ranking of type of migrants in the period leading up to 1990 and the one following (see Figure 2.5). In both periods, the largest group were shuttle migrants, followed by settled migrants. In fact, the proportion of shuttle migrants did undergo change and

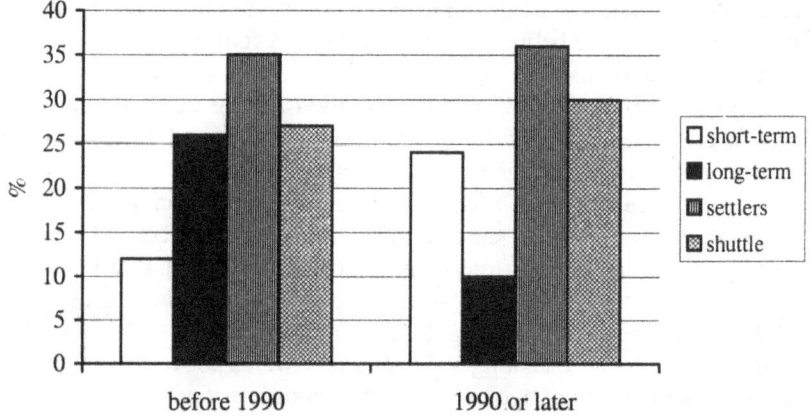

Source: Iglicka, 1998a, p. 92

Figure 2.5 Share of different types of migrants, whole territory

was close to 35 per cent, whereas the share of settled migrants displayed a slight increase (by 3 per cent). The relative frequencies of the remaining two types, however, changed considerably. The share of short-term migrants doubled, boosting this type of migrant from last (fourth) to third place, while the share of long-term migrants declined by more than a half, making those migrants' category in the least numerous since 1989. I consider this change as the most important one in Poles' migratory behaviours during the transition period.

We can observe that relatively short migrations continue to be the most frequent type in the 1990s (see Figure 2.5), even though (and in striking contrast to the recent past) the exchange rate for foreign currency is no longer artificially high in Poland, meaning, for example, the average three-month earnings of a seasonal Polish worker in the West can no longer buy a car in Poland, and the consumer market is in equilibrium. Still, for certain segments of the Polish society, seasonal work and frugal living abroad remain a relatively fast and simple way to improve their standard of living and to acquire superior and fashionable consumer goods. It should also be borne in mind that the 1990s saw the emergence of mass unemployment in Poland. Among those most affected, in addition to fairly old people who proved unable to adapt themselves to market requirements, were young people, particularly vocational school graduates. Some of the unemployed are likely to take part in shuttle or short-term migrations while some others quit their jobs or (in the case of school leavers) do not look for a job in

Poland, often registering as unemployed, precisely because they expect to find a job abroad or are between short-term foreign contracts.

Neither educational attainment nor marital status (at the time of the household survey) caused any serious variation among the basic types of migrants. However, such a differentiating role was played by age (at the time of migration) and, though to a lesser degree, by sex.

Overall, male migrants predominated in the four communes. They constituted 70 per cent of short-term migrants, 65 per cent of shuttle migrants, and 56 per cent of long-term migrants. Among shuttle migrants, young and very young (under 25 years) respondents were most numerous. As far as the selectivity among long-term migrants is concerned, the tendency seems to be that long-term migrants were, above all, relatively older persons (40 years of age or more); they constituted as much as 40 per cent of the total. On the other hand, data from the survey indicate that short-term migration involved various segments regardless of age.

A strikingly uniform tendency in the four communities is a female predominance among the settled migrants. They constituted nearly 55 per cent of all settled migrants. As a rule, those women were either very young (less than 25) or in middle- or late-middle age (40+). This tendency seems to point to a family aspect to the migration, which was also reflected in the official statistics of international migration in Poland until 1994. This may mean that, in many instances, female settlers continue to follow their menfolk, who typically migrate first and usually illegally (Iglicka 2000a).

As far as country of destination is concerned, in the case of first migration and settlement, survey results confirm official data (see Tables 2.13

Table 2.13 Migrants from each of the communes sampled by the first migration destination, 1994-1995 (%)

First migration's destination	Commune of origin			
	Lubniany	Monki	Namyslow	Perlejewo
Germany	96.6	15.0	47.0	2.0
USA	–	44.4	1.8	24.3
Belgium	–	10.6	1.2	63.8
Former Communist Bloc's Countries	1.7	5.0	22.3	4.6
Others	1.7	25.0	27.7	5.3
Total	100.0	100.0	100.0	100.0
Absolute numbers	179	160	170	152

Source: Household survey

and 2.14). In both cases, Germany was in first place, followed by the USA and Belgium.

Table 2.14 Settler migrants from each of the communes sampled by the country of destination, 1994-1995 (%)

Country of destination	Commune of origin			
	Lubniany	Monki	Namyslow	Perlejewo
Belgium	–	13.0	–	73.5
Canada	–	–	11.8	–
Germany	97.7	–	58.8	–
Netherlands	2.3	–	–	–
USA	–	76.1	–	26.5
Other	–	10.9	29.4	–
Total	100.0	100.0	100.0	100.0
Absolute numbers	88	46	17	34

Source: Household survey

Conclusions

The ethnosurvey's findings largely confirm trends observed in the official statistics and help to explain their mechanisms. The most important fact arising from in-depth studies on Poles' mobility is that the main categories of mobility, i.e. shuttle and permanent migration, remained constant through the transition period. The rapid decline of long-term migration (longer than one year) and a sudden rise of short-term migration (from 3 months to 1 year) seem to be harbingers of change in features of mobility. Clearly, the introduction of more restrictive immigration policies in Western Europe, which means limited chances of obtaining work and/or residence permits, and the fact that the cost of living is still more expensive there also induce return to homeland. "The way in which households or individual migrants responded to the situation and to changes in Poland was, to a large degree, differentiated, not only across communes but also within them. The reasons for this are rooted in the demographic, economic and social characteristics of households, as well as in the attitudes of their individual members" (Lukowski, 1998, p. 148). International migration still seems to be a means to accumulate goods and money. However, it is becoming a way of life for some specific segments of society: older, less educated persons who were unable to adapt to Poland's new market economy and young people, mainly vocational school graduates, sometimes unemployed or in the process of seeking a job in Poland.

Mechanisms of Income-Generating Migration Before and During the Transition Period

As previously mentioned, the deficiency of the official data is striking when comparing Polish statistics on emigration and receiving countries' immigration figures. Serious under-estimates occur in Polish sources. A very good example of the deficiency of Polish statistics (and an example pertaining very well to the subject of this chapter) is a comparison of legal and illegal migrants by major destination (see Table 2.15 and Table 2.16).

Table 2.15 Legal migrants by major destination, Poland, 1981-1992 (%)

Destination	1981-1988	1989	1990	1991	1992
Europe total	82.6	81.8	75.2	79.8	80.0
Austria	4.7	2.0	1.0	1.5	1.4
France	3.7	2.0	2.2	1.6	1.5
FRG	58.2	69.8	62.0	69.1	71.0
Greece	a	0.8	0.8	0.9	0.5
Italy	4.0	1.3	1.0	1.1	0.5
Sweden	a	2.0	2.6	2.2	1.6
United Kingdom	1.5	0.7	0.5	0.6	0.4
Europe-other	10.5	3.2	4.3	2.9	3.2
Former USSR	0.3	0.1	0.1	0.1	0.1
Asia	b	0.3	0.3	0.2	0.2
Africa	b	0.3	0.3	0.5	0.4
North America	12.7	16.3	22.1	17.7	17.6
Canada	3.1	5.9	8.6	7.4	6.8
United States	9.6	10.4	13.5	10.3	10.8
South America	b	1.1	0.1	0.1	–
Australia	1.5	1.1	1.8	1.5	1.5
Other	2.9	–	–	–	–
Total	100.0	100.0	100.0	100.0	100.0

a: Included in 'Europe – other'
b: Included in 'other'

Source: Central Statistical Office, Warsaw

In official statistics, emigration to Greece in the 1980s was so low that it was included in the category of "other European countries" and Italy was ranked third. However, in the data extracted from police passports records and illustrating illegal (unregistered) outflow, Greece held fourth place and Italy second (right after the Federal Republic of Germany). So the discrepancies (especially in the case of Greece) are significant.

The following sections analyse the changes in strategies and mechanisms of income-generating migration. Finally, an explanation is given as to why sending and destination areas for this kind of migration changed suddenly towards the end of the 1980s. The majority of findings enclosed in this chapter stem, once again, from the results of the ISS UW survey on causes and consequences of migration from Poland.

Table 2.16 Illegal net emigrants by major country of destination, Poland, 1 April 1981 to 31 December 1988*

Destination	Thousands	Per cent of total
Europe		
Austria	24.5	4.6
France	23.3	4.4
FRG (with West Berlin)	267.8	50.2
Greece	19.6	3.7
Italy	30.3	5.7
United Kingdom	9.6	1.8
Non-European countries		
Australia	4.0	0.7
Canada	14.4	2.7
United States	76.8	14.4
Other	62.7	11.8
Total	533.0	100.0

* Only those who failed to return home by 23 November 1989

Source: Government Population Commission, extracted from police passport records (SERP), Warsaw

Since the early 1970s, Polish migrants were – due to a relatively lenient state policy that allowed for tourist trips abroad – some of the pioneers of income-generating international migration from the CEE region. Within a relative short period of time, the earnings generated from "tourist" trips abroad (which were, in fact, trips by petty-traders or seasonal workers) became an important source of income and consumer goods for tens of thousands and later for hundreds of thousands of Polish households, though a considerable part of such income was undocumented and "hidden." Slowly, part of this mobility converted into longer (but unregistered) stays abroad. Migrants' cumulative experience allowed them to gradually set up their niches in particular local foreign labour markets or to indefinitely extend their independent economic activities there.

Contrary to the trends observed earlier, the main strategy of the income-generating migrations changed radically after the collapse of the communist system. It is now more to maintain the standard of living than to accumulate wealth or enhance migrants' level of consumption. This thesis will be elaborated further on.

As mentioned before, the transformation of the political-economic system brought new developments, challenges and opportunities for a quite large part of the society (especially for younger cohorts of urban professionals). Before the collapse of the system, this group was especially prone to migrate. Positive changes in the quality of life for these people caused official human outflow from Poland to drop significantly after 1989 and reach its lowest level since 1960 (with the small exception of the 1970-1974 period) (see Figure 2.1). However, transition brought also economic hardship and caused such negative phenomena as:

- unemployment,
- difficulties with self-adaptation to market requirements,
- a lack of security among some segments of the society (especially the working class and the rural, middle-aged and poorly-educated).

These influenced the changes in migration patterns after the collapse of the system. The social and economic changes in the wake of the transition of the system also caused short or long-term income-generating emigration from Poland to become the domain of poorly educated segments of the society, i.e. those who could not adapt to the market economy. In the past, they had been less prone to migrate because of the social safety net and lack of unemployment. The strategies of the short or long-term migration continue to include:

- to preserve the existing level of consumption in the country of origin,
- to save up in order to set up some commercial activities back home,
- to enhance the standard of living after returning home.

The first strategy was most common during the transition period. In fact, in today's market economy, the realisation of this strategy is actually contributing to the stagnation in the borderland regions of northeast Poland. This strategy is carried out mainly by short or long-term trips to such western and southern European countries as Belgium, Italy and Greece. The latter two strategies are realised more often by long-term migration to Germany or the USA.

People who are involved in income-generating migrations are mainly inhabitants of backward rural areas and small towns from north- or southeastern regions of Poland. In the case of those headed to Italy, it is people mainly from the former voivodships of Lomza, Bialystok and Suwalki.[14] In the case of Greece it is inhabitants of the former Lomza, Bialystok, Lublin and Przemysl voivodships (Cieslinska, 1992; Romaniszyn, 1996). These have never been typical sending areas. International migration became intensive from these places only with the collapse of the system. Apart from push and pull factors on the macro level, some changes in locals' system of values were also probably conducive to the growth of migration. Namely, it turned out that, in the majority of cases, jobs in domestic service in a nearby town are perceived as dishonourable whereas it is not an embarrassment – according to the respondents – to be a housekeeper or a babysitter in Rome or Athens (ISS UW study). The other interesting characteristic of the transition period is fact that, among those migrants, older cohorts, i.e. those aged 35-39 and 40-44, dominate over younger ones.

The results of the aforementioned in-depth study on migration in Poland enabled the recognition of several basic changes in mechanisms and patterns of short-term and long-term income-generating migration from selected, mainly eastern, regions in Poland during the transition period. These changes are as follows (Lukowski, 1998):

- from long-term migration to Germany or overseas destinations – the USA or Canada – to long – or short-term migration to other the European countries (Belgium, Italy, Greece),
- from accumulation to consumption,
- from periphery to periphery,
- infrequent, though probably increasing chain-migrations of women – indicating a weakening of traditional family ties,
- towards the increase of the autarchic circles of family and neighbours and the marginalisation of the public sphere.

Due to the revaluation of the zloty, the relationship between the initial expenditure for migration (financial and intangible costs, e.g. travel expense, separation from family, discontinuity of job in the country of origin) and the expected profit from it lessened (Lukowski, 1998).

Therefore, migration to the European countries is more affordable than an overseas sojourn; travel is simply much cheaper and more convenient (especially with many new international coach lines).

Until the collapse of the system, the buying power of hard currency made a trip abroad represent an opportunity for a radical change in a family's standard of living. Families earning foreign incomes were able, in a very short time, to improve their economic status considerably. To some degree, going abroad to improve one's material standing became a "normal" activity, and one not necessarily determined by socio-demographic or cultural factors (Lukowski, 1998, p. 147). Now it has changed and remittances from migration are mainly a means to preserve an existing level of consumption. Additionally, earnings from abroad are rarely a source of positive, qualitative changes at the permanent place of residence. If they do, it is mainly the cases of long-term emigration to the USA or those migrating to Germany.

However, in a few cases of emigrants to Belgium, Italy or Greece, it was possible to observe a connection between migrations abroad and internal migrations. Namely, migration abroad preceded internal migration. Interviews with respondents showed migration abroad implied temporary residence on ethnic, cultural and economic peripheries. The internal migrations that followed were movements to the peripheries of large cities (chiefly Warsaw). These peripheries were, in a way, the ultimate destination but there were significant differences between the lifestyle of Poles in immigrant neighbourhoods abroad and their lifestyle on the outskirts of the Warsaw metropolitan area. A considerable proportion of the "return migrants" started to set up their own businesses in the service industry. This is a positive, qualitative change compared to their work abroad and two strategies, namely to accumulate capital in order to get into business in Poland and to enhance the standard of living upon returning home, were accomplished. Again, this pattern of households' strategy was more apparent in cases of return migration from Germany or the USA (Lukowski, 1998).

Currently, journeys to European countries, especially Belgium, Italy and Greece, are increasingly made by women. In many cases, it is not only a migration of a wife (a mother) but also part of a chain-migration of women within one or two nuclear families. In order to ensure the continuance a job abroad and maintain income from it, a mother is "replaced" or "filled in for" by a sister, oldest daughter, etc. A particular kind of tension develops in migrant families in which it is the women who migrate: the men who stay behind have great difficulty taking on traditional female responsibilities. The result is often the negligence of traditional male responsibilities, including providing financial security (Lukowski,

1998). There was also alcoholism and the children's perception of a lack of security was observed. The migration of women is, in a way, a trap that often ends up with the break-up of a family.

One of the most serious consequences of migration is the creation of autarchic circles of family and neighbours and the marginalisation of the public sphere. In local communities within backward and peripheral areas of Poland, the marginalisation of the public sphere reached an advanced level in the 1990s. Residents eligible to vote failed to do so. They do not want to run for public office since such a position would encumber their working abroad. There is also not much demand for the social and welfare services provided by the state and local governments (one exception is the eager acceptance of unemployment benefits in Poland while working abroad) (Lukowski, 1998, p. 147).

Southern European Countries – New Destination Areas

During the last twenty years, all southern European countries have undergone major socio-economic changes, as they have evolved from being countries of emigration to countries of large-scale immigration (Tsoukala, 1999, p. 109). The shift arose most of all from a growth in demand for cheap, unskilled jobs on the secondary labour markets of southern economies, and secondly because of the more strict immigration control in northern European countries. Therefore, while at the beginning of the 1980s most migrants in southern countries were in transit, at the end of the 1980s they had begun to stay there longer mainly because they could be easily employed in the underground economy, which is traditionally more prevalent in southern European countries (Tsoukala, 1999).

The seeming paradox of southern European countries attracting immigrants at the same time as there were high rates of unemployment, especially youth unemployment, is resolved by the fact that most immigrants have established themselves in sectors of the labour market relatively uncontested for by local workers (Golini et al., 1991, p. 257). Many young, local people prefer to remain unemployed well into their late 20s rather than take on "undesirable" jobs that would reflect badly on the prestige of the family (King and Rybaczuk, 1993, p. 184).

Although in keeping with this general pattern of immigration to southern countries, there were two further, major causes of the sudden, unexpected and historically anomalous increase of Polish emigration to Italy and Greece in the 1980s and the 1990s:

- Economic and political crisis in Poland at the beginning of the 1980s and the positive way Italian and Greek governments treated political refugees at that time;

- Economic recession and, as a result, a surplus of local and foreign manpower in the majority of Western European countries, thereby creating difficulties in finding employment (legal or illegal) on the Western European labour markets that had traditionally absorbed Polish migrants such as: Germany, Britain and France.

The first larger wave of Poles to Italy occurred in 1981, following the imposition of martial law in Poland. About two thousand Poles stayed in Italy during that time, all of whom emigrated on to the USA and Canada within a couple of years. In 1983, the next wave of refugees from Poland arrived, increasing the number of Poles in Italy. The turning point in the history of flux of Poles in Italy took place in 1987, when the number of Polish emigrants shot up rapidly. A catalyst for this migratory wave was probably the opportunity to buy vouchers for camping in Italy in Polish zloty. One should realise that the zloty was not convertible at that time and access to hard currencies was banned and very difficult at the end of the 1980s. Therefore, due to this internal hurdle, tourist trips abroad were not easy. However, thanks to the possibility of buying vouchers in Polish zloty, as many as 95 per cent of Polish migrants made it to Italy as tourists. As observed by Ascoli (1986, p. 203):

> Aside from the labour market factor, the attractiveness of Italy also derives from the ease of entering the country. Part of the problem here is the inherent conflict between Italy's desire to be as 'open' as possible to incoming tourists and the fact that entry as a tourist is one of the easiest paths for potential illegal workers to come and find work.

This was obviously a favourable factor for the increase in Polish migrants in the 1980s. The inflow of Polish "tourists" kept up; according to the Polish Embassy, there were 13 thousand Polish emigrants at the end of the 1980s. According to Polish Church estimates, this population exceeded 14 thousand. Twelve thousand of them had refugee status, the rest stayed illegally (Iglicka, Barsotti and Lecchini, 1999b).

Emigration to Italy in the 1980s originated mainly from urban regions. Women made up somewhere between 54 and 61 per cent of the total number. Although big in numbers, Poles did not form an integrated community at the end of the 1980s. According to Cieslinska (1992), the majority of them expected further emigration and, in fact, most of them had emigrated onward from Italy by the beginning of the 1990s. In point of fact, the number of Poles in Italy during the 1980s had to be much higher than either the embassy's or the Church's estimate since, despite the constant outflow, the number of Poles holding the residence permit (*permesso di soggiorno*) tallied 18,860 in 1991.[15]

Since the early 1990s, the number of Poles migrating to Italy has grown significantly. However, the mechanisms of this migration have altered. The results of the in-depth qualitative studies on migration from Poland to Italy indicate the emergence of a new type of migration, namely income-generating seasonal migration besides the short- and long-term ones (Cieslinska, 1992). This new type of migration probably started at the end of the 1980s and coincided with the demand for a cheap foreign labour on Italian secondary labour markets. Migrants from Poland have been finding employment mainly in two niches of the grey economy. They work, for the most part, in construction and in the service sector (transport, cleaning services, hotels and catering). They are concentrated in Rome.

A Polish network has already been established, which encourages migration. In the study conducted by the ISS UW, the so-called the "parish network" is mentioned by interviewees as a very important institution for, on the one hand, promoting a sense of security among migrants but, on the other, limiting intercultural communication (Lukowski, 1998). This is very true in the case of Italy where the massive presence of Polish clergy, which came on the heels of the election of a Pole as Pope, was conducive to the development of a very strong migrants' network, with the Church acting as a channel (Iglicka, Barsotti and Lecchini, 1999b).

The first larger flux of Poles into Greece took place in 1981 after the introduction of martial law in Poland. About one thousand Poles stayed in Greece during that time. All of them seem to have further emigrated to Australia, USA and Canada by the end of the 1980s. None-the-less, the institutions they established, parishes, schools and newspapers, set the basis for subsequent waves of migrants. Due to the cultural infrastructure and the emergence of a large demand in secondary sectors of the Greek economy for cheap foreign labour, the number of Poles migrating to Greece started to grow significantly. The demand for foreigners was especially visible in the private sector and encouraged short- and long-term outflows from Poland (Romaniszyn 1996, 1997).

According to Greek statistics, there were 13,300 Poles staying legally in Greece in 1991. According to the estimates of the Greek Ministry of Labour, the total number of Poles in Greece, whether legally or illegally, oscillated at around 60,000 in the mid-1990s. During the regularisation program conducted between January 1998 and April 1999, of a total of 374,000 applications for regularisation, about 8,000 Poles obtained a white card (a temporary permit) – the first stage to being granted a green card (a permanent permit). This ranked Poles sixth (after Albanians, Egyptians, Bulgarians, Pakistanis and Romanians) among foreigners legalising their residence in Greece (OECD, 1999).

Two kinds of Polish illegal workers go to Greece: permanent illegal workers and seasonal workers. "Permanent" illegals stay illegally in Greece for even as long as 3-4 years. They generally find employment in two niches of the grey economy: construction and domestic service, primarily in Athens. Contrary to this, seasonal workers are scattered among the islands. They work mainly in the tourist industry: in hotels and restaurant as chambermaids, cleaners or waiters and in farming as harvesters or agricultural labourers. Generally, Poles are hired mainly as "land" workers, few work in the sea industry (Romaniszyn, 1997).

Conclusions

Poles' Mediterranean-bound income-generating migration in the 1990s was a result of factors conducive to emigration in the country of origin and favourable conditions in the receiving areas. The underlying push factor was the economic hardship brought by the political, economic and social transformation borne by some segments of the Polish society that inclined them to see migration abroad as the only way to preserve their existing level of consumption. Contributing factors were economic recession and the resulting surplus of local and foreign manpower in most Western European countries that impeded finding employment (legal or illegal) on the Western European labour markets that were traditional for Polish migrants, such as Germany, Britain and France. Favourable conditions for illegal and cheap foreign labour were found in Italy and Greece, e.g. the high seasonality of these economies (especially in construction, tourism and agriculture), and the continuing exodus of Italians and Greeks from low-status jobs. These factors created a huge demand for foreign labour in the secondary labour market, in which Poles found their niches.

Because of their geographic position and their long tradition of welcoming people in flight, Italy and Greece receive refugees in transit to third countries and others who seek asylum. From the historical perspective, both Italy and Greece have never been major destination for Polish migrants (OECD, 1999). The significant migratory-relationship between Poles and these two countries started in 1981 when the Polish communist government introduced martial law. Thousands of refugees and asylum seekers found shelter and welcome, and thus security, in these two countries. Some of them spent years there waiting for their turn for overseas migration. Then, at the end of the 1980s and due to the co-existence of pull and push factors, a phenomenon described by Massey (1999, p. 306) took place. According to him, there was a strong tendency to continue the original migratory stream because of the growth and development of migrant networks. The concentration of immigrants in certain destination areas creates a "family and friends" effect that channels later streams of immigrants to the same place and eases their arrival and integration. Finally, a sufficiently large number of migrants is conducive to the formation of an enclave economy, thereby increasing the demand for immigrant workers.

Polish migrants arriving in Italy and Greece originate from rural, backward regions in eastern Poland. Their destinations are the big metropolises of Rome and Athens. It is a migration of poorly educated people past their youth (the middle groups of productive age predominate), mostly those who could not adapt to the market economy back home. Their migration exacerbates the economic and social stagnation in the sending areas.

It is difficult to predict the future size of the Mediterranean-bound flow of Poles. It depends on economic conditions in Poland, the Italian and Greek governments' immigration policy but mostly on the demand of the Italian and Greek economies for foreign labour. After all, the history of the post-war European migration proves that economic migration takes place when demographic pressures in one country are met by a corresponding readiness of markets to receive workers in another.

Notes

1   Some fragments of these sections were published in Polish, see Iglicka 1998b.
2   The change of registered permanent address in connection with moving abroad signifies, in practice, a permanent migration. It is now, as in the past, the sole type of migration officially noted in Poland. According to the definition of migration adopted in Poland, "emigration" is the notification of the authorities of a change of one's permanent address in connection with leaving Poland to take up residence abroad, and "immigration" is the registration at a permanent address if the former residence was abroad. Temporary international migrations have not, as a rule, been recorded in Polish statistics. In the 1980s, the scale of migration from Poland could be estimated on the basis of the Passport Traffic Registration System (SERP), which was abolished in 1989. Under that system, all individuals applying for permission to travel abroad were registered, statistics on border crossings were collected and returns were recorded.
3   On 1 February, 1952, an agreement was signed between the authorities of the Polish People's Republic and the German Democratic Republic, under which the individuals who had not yet acquired Polish citizenship were to move to East Germany.
4   An agreement between the Red Cross organisations concerned the cases of family reunions involving the closet relatives, as well as special cases, such as lone old age and disability. The criteria for emigration agreed between the Polish and the German Red Cross organisations precluded, in principle, emigration by individuals who had acquired Polish citizenship through a certificate of belonging to the Polish people, despite having ascendants or descendants in West Germany, if their livelihood was provided for in Poland (Lempinski, 1987).
5   An inspection in the Szczecin voivodship revealed that, in 1957, about 60 per cent of the investigated cases of emigration from this voivodship did not meet the emigration permit qualification criteria in force at that time. The laxity even induced individuals and families resident in other voivodships to resettle there in order to seek permission to emigrate to Germany (Lempinski, 1987).

6   The proportion of children up to the age of 13 increased to 31 per cent in 1956, compared to 12 per cent in the preceding year (and continued at that level up to 1960) (Latuch, 1961).
7   The *Notification by the Government of the Polish People's Republic* was a component of the agreements between the Polish and German governments comprising a treaty signed by the two states on December 7th, 1970. The treaty was the starting point for the process of normalisation of relations between the Polish People's Republic and the Federal Republic of Germany; it provided a legal and political basis for the resolution of the existing problems and disputes and for the arrangement of mutual relations in a way that would both suit the interests of the two states and serve détente in Europe.
8   Under these criteria, those eligible for emigration comprised: 1) individuals who "indisputably belonged to the German nation." However, the Notification did not explain how the term "indisputable German nationality" should be understood. The decision-making expert commissions took into consideration the language, the nationality of the parents of the individuals concerned, as well as the national character of schools they had attended prior to 1945, p. 2) a certain number of people from mixed families, among whom the sense of belonging to the German people had prevailed over the past years; 3) divided families: according to the Polish signatory, the family reunion principle applied to parents, grandparents, descendants, spouses, and certain individuals in extremely difficult situations. According to the German party the principle was applicable to: relatives in a direct line, wives, husbands, siblings, including married siblings, which meant that mixed couples were able to migrate to the Federal Republic of Germany, and, in special cases, more distant relatives as well; 4) those Polish citizens who expressed a wish to be reunited with their close relatives resident in East Germany or West Germany as a result of changes of relations within their families (Lempinski, 1987).
9   The subject of negotiations under the provision was a group of people "regarded by Poland as its own citizens and viewed by Germany as a group of German nationality" (Lempinski, 1987).
10 The provision extended the circle of the eligible to include "the individuals who had already filed applications for emigration and whose closest relatives, family members, spouses and/or descendants have, for various reasons, not returned from the Federal Republic of Germany to their families in Poland" (Lempinski, 1987).
11 It was not until late 1983 that the regulations governing emigration policy to the Federal Republic of Germany were changed. Persons emigrating permanently to that state now retain their Polish citizenship, and may renounce it on the territory of the Federal Republic of Germany by applying at Polish Embassy in the Federal Republic of Germany.
12 For the sake of comparison, the proportion of Poles in the total migration inflow into Germany between 1980 and 1989 was 17 per cent (Slany, 1991).
13 The greatest numbers of people emigrated permanently from the Katowice, Opole and Gdansk voivodships.
14 According to the administrative division of the country prior to 1999.
15 Ministry of the Interior data.

References

Ascoli, U. (1986), 'Migration of workers and the labour market: is Italy becoming a country of immigration?', in R. Rogers (ed) *Guests come to stay*, Westview, Boulder.
Cieslinska, B. (1992), 'Polacy we Wloszech' (Poles in Italy), *Wiadomosci Socjologiczne*, no. 2, pp. 43-61.

German Statistical Office data (1995), direct communications to UN/ECE secretariat.
Golini, A., Gesano, G. and Heins, G. (1991), 'South-North migration with special reference to Europe', *International Migration*, vol. 29, no. 2, pp. 253-77.
Government Population Commission (1989) data, Warsaw.
Heffner, K. (1999), 'The Return of Emigrants from Germany to Upper Silesia: Reality and Prospects', in K. Iglicka and K. Sword (eds), *The Challenge of East-West Migration for Poland*, Macmillan, London.
Hryniewicz, J., Jalowiecki, B. and Myne, A. (1992), *The Brain Drain in Poland*, University of Warsaw Press, Warsaw.
Iglicka, K. (1998a), 'Current migratory patterns', in T. Frejka, M. Okolski and K. Sword (eds), *In-depth studies on migration in Central and Eastern Europe: The case of Poland*, UN, New York, Geneva, pp. 57-69.
Iglicka, K. (1998b), *Analiza zachowan migracyjnych na podstawie wynikow badania etnosondazowego migracji zagranicznych w wybranych regionach Polski w latach 1975-1994* (Analysis of migratory behaviours on selected regions of Poland, 1975-1994 – ethnosurvey results), SGH Press, Warsaw.
Iglicka, K. (2000a), 'Mechanisms of migration from Poland before and during the transition period', *Journal of Ethnic and Migration Studies*, vol. 26, no. 1, pp. 61-73.
Iglicka, K., Barsotti, O. and Lecchini, L. (1999), *Recent Development of Migration From Poland to Europe with a Special Emphasis on Italy. Le migrazioni est-ovest. Le unioni miste in Italia*, Universita di Pisa, report no 131, Pisa.
Iglicka, K., Jazwinska, E. and Okolski, M. (1996), 'Wspolczesne migracje zagraniczne ludnosci Polski. Badania za pomoca podejscia etnosondazowego' (Contemporary international migration of Poles. An ethnosurvey study), *Studia Demograficzne*, no. 4, pp. 3-41.
Kersten, K. (1974), *Repatriacja ludnosci Polski po drugiej wojnie swiatowej* (Repatriation of Polish Population after the Second World War), University of Wroclaw Press, Wroclaw.
King, R. and K. Rybaczuk (1993), 'Southern Europe and the international division of labour: from emigration to immigration', in R. King (ed), *The New Geography of European Migrations*, Belharen Press, London.
Kurcz, Z. (2000), 'The German Minority in Poland after 1945', in F.E.I. Hamilton and K. Iglicka (eds), *From Homogeneity to Multiculuralism. Minorities Old and New in Poland*, SSEES, University of London, London.
Latuch, M. (1961), *Repatriacja ludnosci Polski w latach 1955-1960 na tle ruchow wedrowkowych* (Repatriation of Polish population in the light of population mobility in the country), SGPiS Press, Warsaw.
Lempinski, Z. (1987), *RFN wobec problemow ludnosciowych w stosunkach z Polska, 1970-1985* (Federal Republic of Germany on population in relations with Poland), Slaski Instytut Naukowy, Katowice.
Lukowski, W. (1998), 'A "Pendular Society": Hypotheses Based On In-Depth Interviews and Qualitative Research', in T. Frejka, M. Okolski and K. Sword (eds), *In-Depth Studies on Migration in Central and Eastern Europe: The Case of Poland*, UN, New York and Geneva, pp. 145-53.
Massey, D.S. (1987), 'The Ethnosurvey in Theory and Practise', *International Migration Review*, vol. 21, no. 4, pp. 1498-522.
Massey, D.S. (1999), 'International Migration at the Dawn of the Twenty-first Century: The Role of the State', *Population and Development Review*, vol. 25, no. 2, pp. 303-22.
OECD (1999), *Trends in International Migration*, SOPEMI report, OECD, Paris.
Okolski, M. (1994), 'Poland', in S. Ardittis (ed), *The Politics of East-West Migration*, St. Martin's Press, New York.

Okolski, M. (1998b), 'A profile of the communities', in T. Frejka, M. Okolski and K. Sword (eds), *In-depth studies on migration in Central and Eastern Europe: The case of Poland*, UN, New York, Geneva, pp. 189-217.

Pilch, A. and Zgorniak, M. (eds) (1984), *Emigracja z ziem polskich w czasach nowozytnych i najnowszych* (Emigration from Polish lands in modern and contemporary times), PWN, Warsaw.

Pries, L. (ed) (1999), *Migration and Transnational Social Spaces*, Ashgate, Aldershot.

Rocznik Demograficzny (Demographic Yearbook) (1998), Central Statistical Office, Warsaw.

Rocznik Statystyczny (Statistical Yearbook) (1995), Central Statistical Office, Warsaw.

Romaniszyn, K. (1996), 'Polacy w Grecji' (Poles in Greece), *Studia Polonijne*, vol. 16, pp. 7-98.

Romaniszyn, K. (1997), 'Wspolczesna nielegalna migracja zarobkowa z Polski do Grecji w perspektywie procesu integracji Europy' (Recent illegal income-generating migration from Poland to Greece in the light of the process of European Integration), in J.E. Zamojski (ed), *Migracje i Spoleczenstwo*, vol. 2, pp. 153-63.

Slany, K. (1991), 'Emigracja z Polski w latach 1980 do glownych krajow emigracji zamorskiej i kontynentalnej: aspekty demograficzno-spoleczne' (Emigration from Poland to the main countries of destination in the 1980s: demographic and social aspects), *Przeglad Polonijny*, no. 4, pp. 15-36.

Slany, K. (ed) (1997), Emigracyjne orientacje Polakow (Emigrational Orientation of Poles), UJ, Krakow.

Stola, D. (forthcoming), 'Migrations in Central Europe: Poland', in C. Wallace and D. Stola (eds), *Central Europe: The New Migration Space*, Macmillan, London.

Tsoukala, A. (1999), 'The perception of the "other" and the integration of immigrants in Greece', in A. Geddes and A. Favell (eds), *The Politics of Belonging: Migrants and Minorities in Contemporary Europe*, Ashgate, Aldershot, pp. 109-23.

Wasilewska-Trenkner, M. (1973), *Ekonomiczno-spoleczne aspekty emigracji z Polski w latach 1960-1965* (Economic and social aspects of emigration from Poland, 1960-1965), WES SGPiS Press, Warsaw.

3 Mobility from Poland's East

Introduction

For more than 30 years, immigration has been one of the most advantageous factors and a power behind economic restructuring throughout the world. Western Europe has ceased to be a sending area for overseas destinations and most of its countries have turned into immigrant-receiving areas. "By the 1980s, even traditional sending countries in southern Europe such as Italy, Spain, and Portugal began to import workers from Africa, Asia and the Middle East. Most of the world's developed countries have become diverse, multiethnic societies, and those that have not reached this stage are moving decisively in that direction" (Massey et al., 1993, p. 443).

At the end of the 1980s, the transformation of the political and economic structure of the CEE region disturbed what had been stable migration trends. Although Poland is still a country whose net migration outflow is higher than its influx (see Figure 3.1), new quantitative and qualitative changes such as an increase in foreigners granted residency, the growth of labour migration, the formation of immigrant communities and the creation of immigrant niches on labour markets – processes that inevitably accompany increased immigration – has led some policy makers and academics to state that Poland is slowly becoming a net-immigration and transit country (Korcelli, 1991; Salt, 1996; Iglicka and Sword, 1999; Kozlowski, 1999; Hamilton and Iglicka, 2000).

One of the most important factors that initiated the unsettling of rather stable migration patterns in the Central Europe was movements from the former Soviet Union. The character and scale of this population flow took everyone by surprise. Researchers still today have a problem with defining this phenomenon since it fails to fulfil two basic criteria usually inherent in the definition of migration, i.e. the legality (or registrability) of flow and a minimum (intended or actual) duration of stay (or permission to stay for a certain time-span). In other literature on CEE population trends, it has been called "petty-trade migration," "shuttle mobility," "circular migration" and "incomplete migration" (Morokvasic and de Tinguy, 1993; Okolski, 1998c; 1999; Wallace and Stola, forthcoming). It is proposed here to term it *primitive mobility*. In the following section I explain why this expression seems to be the most befitting.

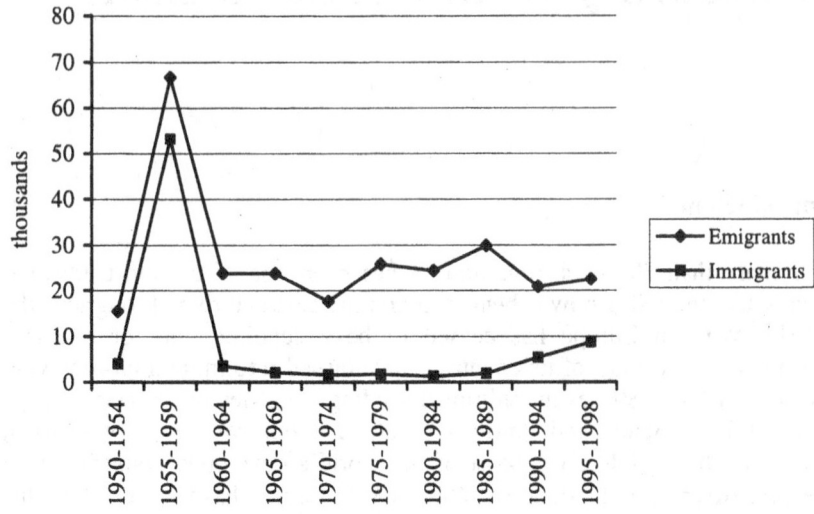

Source: Central Statistical Office

Figure 3.1 Trends in emigration and immigration, Poland 1950-1998

Definition, Statistics and the Scope of the Phenomenon

According to one of the general typologies of migration, there are five broad classes of migration: primitive, forced, impelled, free and mass (Petersen, 1966, p. 54). Contemporary Europe experiences all but one of them. Primitive migration, which denotes a movement related to man's inability to cope with natural forces or shortage of food or water, is not visible.

The kind of shuttle mobility experienced within the Central and Eastern European region since the collapse of communism, characteristic for any transition period and in my opinion bound to be short-lived, may, to some extent and, in the light of the above typology, be classified as primitive, since its root cause was largely a shortage of basic goods. In other words, when systems collapse very old and forgotten types of demographic and social behaviours may revive with a new strength. However, as already mentioned, these renewed mobility behaviours fail to fulfil two basic criteria usually intrinsic in the definition of migration, so this author has suggested using the term *primitive mobility* in lieu of "primitive migration" (Iglicka, 1999b).

It is also important to distinguish this kind of mobility from shuttle migration or cross-border commuting in frontier regions, as often witnessed between Western European countries or in the Americas e.g. France and Germany, France and Switzerland and Mexico and the USA. Inhabitants of frontier regions often shop in a neighbouring country, especially when the prices are lower there, but it is done more for private savings than for resale at a profit. This is also a different phenomenon than the shuttle migration of Poles that took place immediately before the collapse of the communist system in the 1980s. In a majority of cases, the Poles turned to trade during tourist sojourns primarily to cover travel costs and only secondly for profit. What differs people involved in *primitive mobility* between some new, ex-Soviet countries and Poland from other shuttle migrants is the very fact that citizens of the former Soviet Union have become "professionals" in this movement. They often gave up their jobs simply because trading, due to differences in currency exchange rates or prices between the countries, turned out to be much more profitable for them. Therefore, international commuting became their main source of income and *de facto* "job." They spend substantial lengths of time abroad or away from home because of trading and travelling.

> The long hours that traders from the east are prepared to devote to travelling suggests that these people do not count their time as an integral cost of the operation. This lack of regard for time as a resource may be on the one hand a relic of the Soviet period and state control of the economy, on the other hand it may be reflect current conditions in the former Soviet republics – in particular, the cheapness of labour and the shortage of meaningful work there (Sword, 1999, p. 164).

Petty-traders from the former USSR have created a new social phenomenon of people constantly on the move, having left their abandoned families behind (Iglicka, 1999b). Furthermore, the frequency of international movements in the case of *primitive mobility* is very high and the volume of transported products huge.

* * *

The fall of the communist system and the slow and sometimes painful birth of its replacement have generated a phenomenon that was completely unexpected by both people and governments in Western, Central and Eastern Europe, namely the new spatial mobility of citizens of former Soviet bloc countries. At the beginning, this mobility was perceived mainly as a threat. Then it turned out to have many positive effects. As Morokvasic and de Tinguy have pointed out at the beginning of the 1990s;

The most characteristic of the post 1989 migrations, and the least known in the West, are the circulatory migrations or commuting of tourists; these involve various types of income-generating activities, mostly trading. They existed on a limited scale before the fall of the iron curtain. These "tourists" stay for periods ranging from several hours to several months. Given their visibility on street corners and markets, these movements nourish fears of invasion among Central Europeans (Morokvasic and de Tinguy, 1993, pp. 253-4).

Border traffic statistics show that the unexpected geographic population movements resulted in the number of arrivals of foreigners in Poland to soar tenfold between 1989 and 1999 (from 8.2 million to 88.6 million) (see Table 3.1). It is clear that the increase in the cross-border movement by foreigners across Poland's borders was far more dramatic than by Poles themselves. The influx of foreigners from the former Soviet Union was been largely responsible for this growth.

Table 3.1 Departure of Poles and arrivals of foreigners, 1985-1998 (in millions)

Year	Departures of Poles			Arrivals of foreigners			Ratio of departures to arrivals
	Actual number	1985 = 100	Previous year = 100	Actual number	1985 = 100	Previous year = 100	
1985	6.3	100	–	3.4	100	–	188
1986	7.3	114	114	3.8	113	113	191
1987	8.5	133	116	4.7	139	123	179
1988	9.9	155	116	6.2	182	131	159
1989	19.3	302	195	8.2	241	133	235
1990	22.1	346	114	18.2	534	231	121
1991	20.8	325	94	36.8	1080	202	56
1992	29.3	458	141	49.0	1437	133	60
1993	31.4	491	107	60.9	1787	124	52
1994	34.3	535	109	74.4	2178	122	46
1995	36.1	573	105	82.2	2414	110	44
1996	43.5	690	124	87.5	2573	108	49
1997	48.6	771	111	87.8	2582	100	55
1998	49.3	782	101	88.6	2605	101	55

Source: Iglicka, K. (2000b), Polish Border Guard statistics

As far as numbers of visitors from the former Soviet Union are concerned, in 1989 fewer than 3 million of them entered Poland. Their number more than doubled the next year and continued to grow to more than 14 million in the peak year of 1997 (Stola, 2000). In January 1998, Polish authorities complied with commitments arising from the forthcoming European Union (EU) expansion and changed the Aliens Law[1] and regulations on necessary documents for entry to Poland. This immediately affected movements from Belarus and Russia; Ukraine, Latvia, Estonia and Lithuania had already signed new agreements on visa-free travel with Poland. With new, stricter entry regulations[2] and the 1998 Russian economic crisis the numbers dropped; to date (mid-1999) this trend has not been reversed (Stola, 2000).

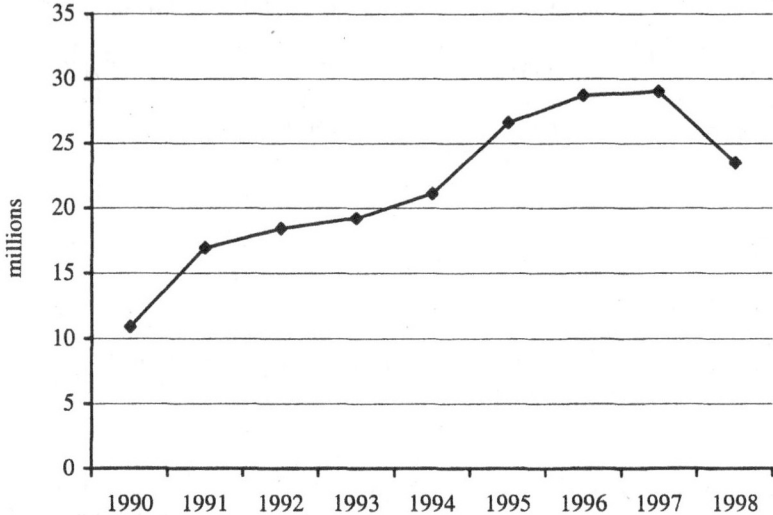

Source: Border Guard Statistics

Figure 3.2 Border crossings on the eastern border, 1990-1998

Citizens of the former Soviet Union arriving in Poland at the beginning of the 1990s did not come here simply to enjoy their recently obtained freedom of movement. Most movements were a side-effect of a sick post-Soviet economy and took the form of "shuttle" mobility, which generally lasted from 3 to 7 days and was mainly trade purposes.

Until 1993, people arriving from the former Soviet Union used to sell cheap, poor-quality goods from their home countries. They returned home with hard currency (i.e. dollars or German marks). Since 1993, when the price relations between Poland and the former Soviet Union changed and selling products made in the former USSR became less profitable, they started to buy goods in Poland for resale in their home countries. Massive purchases of products were made, mainly of clothing, shoes and electronic equipment, which partly offset Poland's chronic, negative official balance of payments.

Table 3.2 The value of expenditures made by foreigners from neighbouring states in Poland, 1994-1996

Country	1994 (in mln PLN*)	1995 (in mln PLN*)	1996 (in mln PLN*)
Belarus	456.9	778.1	1184.7
Czech Republic	421.2	512.5	870.7
Germany	3628.2	4470.1	4965.6
Lithuania	116.4	130.7	118.8
Russia	109.2	84.0	138.9
Slovakia	133.7	160.3	251.3
Ukraine	317.8	578.2	1248.9

* 1 US$ = 2.9–3.4 PLN

Source: Ruch graniczny i wydatki cudzoziemcow w Polsce, 1994-1996. GUS (Central Statistical Office), Warsaw, 1997, p. 23

Besides easy access to Poland, migrants have also had relatively easy access to Poland's informal labour market (Stola, forthcoming). An estimate made on the basis of a 1995 survey conducted in Ukraine and Poland suggests that there may have been more than 500,000 Ukrainians travelling to Poland to work illegally. A great majority of them were petty-traders who, in addition to their trade activities, took up various, usually very short-term employment (Okolski, 1998c).[3] According to the Polish Ministry of Labour and Social Policy, there are about 100,000-150,000 foreigners working illegally each year in Poland (*Informal Labour Market*, 1995). The majority of them come from the "East" (in Poland, this is assumed to include the ex-Soviet countries). Although, according to that estimate, a substantial proportion of those people are seasonal workers, the estimates probably does not include foreigners who are employed for a very short period of time (e.g. for two weeks or less) (Okolski, 1998c).

There were five major factors that contributed to the rapid expansion of spatial mobility of people from the former Soviet Union into Central

Europe. We may list them here as: 1) the economic crisis in the countries of the former Soviet Union, which caused tremendous shortages of basic goods; 2) an overvalued ruble; 3) the geographic proximity between Poland and the former USSR; 4) easy access to the West (Poland); and 5) difficult access to the Western European countries.

As mentioned before, this influx had many positive points. For several years, citizens of the former Soviet Union visiting Poland to shop fostered local economic growth. Foreign demand for textile and leather products was one of the main factors, for instance, behind the boom in small, private clothing and footwear businesses (Okolski, 1996). The Warsaw Bazaar is a very good example of the "international petty-trade" occurring in Poland since the beginning of the 1990s (Sword, 1999). With the growing participation of foreigners from the East (not only citizens of the former Soviet Union but Asians as well – almost 60 per cent of customers at the market are foreigners), the bazaar turned into a huge, predominantly clothing-oriented market place. In 1995, the estimated annual turnover surpassed US$500 million, making the bazaar one of the biggest Polish enterprises in terms of turnover. The Warsaw Bazaar provides direct employment to over

Table 3.3 Purchases made by foreigners at the Polish Bazaars

Bazaar	Foreign customers (% of turnover)	Of which wholesale (%)	Amount (in mln PLN based on 1996 turnover)*
Kostrzyn	93	0	112 (9)
Cedynia	93	0	150 (8)
Slubice	92	0	175 (7)
Cieszyn	91	0	46 (14)
Swinoujscie	88	0	62 (12)
Legnica	87	0.1	348 (4)
Bialystok	83	22	432 (3)
Gubin	82	0	90 (10)
Zgorzelec	80	0	72 (11)
Przemysl	67	10	60 (13)
Warsaw	58	32	870 (1)
Tuszyn	31	29	589 (2)
Rzgow	24	14	204 (6)
Gluchow	19	19	238 (5)
Krakow	1	0	13 (15)

* 1 US$ = 3.4 PLN

Source: Sword, 1999, p. 153

6,500 people. Conservative estimates show that at least 3,000 are foreigners (Kozlowski, 1999). Altogether, the Warsaw Bazaar activities (including factories supplying the fair) are the source of employment for as many as 60,000 people (Okolski, 1996, p. 16). In addition, the Warsaw Bazaar and other open-air markets created for traders from the East act as a training ground and a first step for future entrepreneurs from the former USSR, who will ultimately go on and found more orthodox and established businesses (Sword, 1999, p. 165). "The Warsaw Bazaar, despite being a hive of activity, is only the 'tip of the iceberg' of an extensive trading network which spreads out across Poland, but also across the eastern border. A vast array of smaller town and village markets in Ukraine, Belarus and Lithuania, as well as further afield, are being supplied from the Warsaw Bazaar and the other large Polish bazaars" (Sword, 1999, p. 164).

> Anna: I started to go to Poland, to the town of Chelm, which is close to the border. My trading sideline picked up and I left my job. Although the profits from my trips were not large, they were much greater than my salary as an art critic. Once I met a [Polish] person who was an owner of a small private shop producing practical, small-sized and inexpensive kitchen units. These units were easily assembled and rather compact. So I started to import them. In Kiev, it was not a problem to sell these units through advertising them in the local newspaper. The profits started rising. This allowed me to rent a car to take more units. During my regular cross-border travels I developed good contacts with customs officers and local people. One of them, who used to help to load the furniture, with time became my partner. He bought a truck and started to take furniture directly from the producers to Kiev. Now he can take fifteen kitchen suites altogether and recently we have started transporting upholstered furniture. In one of the Kiev cinemas, which are nowadays closed, I arranged with the managers to exhibit the furniture in the lobby. So now I have a permanent job. When the furniture arrives, I sell it. Now I can avoid these exhausting journeys. I order furniture by phone and my partner brings it. I have only to give him the money (Khomra, 1994, pp. 165-6).

When new, stricter policy regulations towards the flux from the East were introduced in January 1998, sales at big bazaars in eastern and central Poland declined dramatically. The subsequent, intensive lobbying by Polish traders and manufacturers to make the government reconsider certain regulations (Stola, 2000) resulted in a lowering of tourist vouchers prices and of the minimum daily quota of money required for a stay in Poland.

A new and dangerous phenomenon caused by the mass presence of foreigners from the former USSR is crime. This crime is mainly committed on foreigners by foreigners. Visitors from the former Soviet Union arrive in Poland with cash instead of credit cards or cheques and so are easy targets for criminals who, for the most part, are also citizens of the former USSR.

Statistics depicting crime by foreigners do not suggest a large scale phenomenon but they do indicate a growing trend toward more dangerous crimes, e.g. armed robbery and homicide, committed especially by Ukrainians.[4] Thus, whereas in 1992 citizens of the former USSR comprised 17.5 per cent of all foreigners who were charged with a crime and faced judicial proceedings, in 1998 they made up 65.5 per cent, of which 10-20 per cent were charged with serious crimes.

Contrary to other national groups entering Poland from the East, the bulk of Belarussian, Russian and Ukrainian nationals arrested for illegally crossing the Polish border were probably involved in no kind of illegal trans-border activity besides illegal entry and smuggling in aliens. As a matter of fact, with the important exception of people from Moldavia, the incidence of apprehensions of foreigners from Eastern European countries was on decline (Okolski, 1998c). Table 3.4 shows the respective numbers of migrants believed to be major client groups of people-smugglers.

Table 3.4 Trafficked foreigners detained on the borders (major national groups), 1995-1996

Country of origin	1995	1996	Increase (%)
Moldova	639	1,067	67.0
Armenia	1,356	1,010	-25.5
Afghanistan	459	867	88.9
Iraq	372	626	68.3
Sri Lanka	201	609	203.0
India	772	484	-37.3
Pakistan	257	443	72.4
Bangladesh	118	219	85.6

Source: Okolski, 1998c, p. 18

In 1996, local administrative units issued 5,087 deportation orders; this represents a 59 per cent increase over the previous year. As mentioned earlier, in 1998 and 1999 Poland imposed stricter rules and procedures towards irregular or illegal foreigners. This produced largely increased number of decisions to expel unwanted foreigners. The number of such decisions increased from 5,707 in 1997 to as many as 9,000 foreigners in 1998. People from the former USSR were among those most frequently deported, the most common nationalities being Ukrainians, Armenians,

Bulgarians, Romanians, Bangladeshis, Indians, Sri Lankans, Belarussians, Moldavians, Pakistanis and Russians.

Table 3.5 Decisions on expulsion of foreigners taken by district administration* by country of origin. Poland: 1994-1998

Country of origin	1994	1995	1996	1997	1998	1994-1998
Afghanistan	–	25	48	133	151	357
Algeria	53	27	62	24	22	188
Armenia	149	505	606	261	875	2,396
Bangladesh	–	8	280	179	213	680
Belarus	82	128	211	119	278	818
Bulgaria	146	209	432	473	360	1,620
China	–	4	169	37	21	231
Czech Republic	2	6	3	338	5	354
FYR Macedonia	3	32	18	34	66	153
Georgia	24	21	27	44	67	183
India	4	241	327	154	67	793
Iraq	–	10	23	77	71	181
Latvia	38	31	30	28	38	165
Lithuania	39	57	50	84	122	352
Moldova	21	211	357	285	382	1,256
Mongolia	14	14	9	65	97	199
Pakistan	2	47	226	103	151	529
Romania	184	397	561	1,049	1,537	3,728
Russia	151	192	188	110	239	880
Slovakia	2	3	–	114	4	123
Sri Lanka	–	22	273	286	299	880
Turkey	4	10	33	23	55	125
Ukraine	826	815	887	844	1,247	4,619
Vietnam	16	13	45	24	233	331
Yugoslavia	15	25	13	41	83	177
All other	170	279	339	472	1,355	2,615
Total	1,843	3,199	5,087	5,166	7,955	23,250

* i.e. by district administration offices (urzad wojewodzki)

Source: Polish Border Guard statistics; Department for Migration and Refugee Affairs, Ministry of the Interior and Administration

Poland actually expelled over 23,250 foreigners (of whom 4,619 to Ukraine, 3,728 to Romania, 2,396 to Armenia and 1,620 to Bulgaria in 1994-1998).

Survey Results

Trends in shuttle mobility into Poland have been investigated rather thoroughly in some surveys. This author's summer 1995 survey, at Terespol and Medyka, the two biggest border crossings on the eastern Polish border, had almost exclusively a quantitative character. The questionnaire was applied to a random sample of 792 citizens of the former USSR, of whom women were in the majority (56 per cent).[5] Although the sample included a large number of well-educated people (11 per cent of the total sample had graduated with post-secondary education and 19 per cent had an incomplete post secondary education), more than 60 per cent of respondents described themselves as unemployed. Closer questioning revealed that being out of work was often a matter of a personal choice and a strategy for living, since respondents felt that commuting between countries was more financially worthwhile than holding down a regular job in their home countries. Thus, survey results confirm, to some extent, the hypothesis of there being "professionals" in this cross-border activity.

The occupational cross-section of both the employed and the unemployed taken as a whole showed that the largest single group was formed by engineers (16 per cent), followed by teachers (10 per cent). Monthly salaries declared by the respondents were between US$25 and US$230, depending on profession and country of origin. In comparison to this, net profits from one trip to Poland amounted to 40-50 per cent of the expenditures on merchandise and were on average US$790 (for the sub-sample of women) and US$710 (for the sub-sample of men) (Iglicka, 1999a).

The interviewee sample consisted of respondents of nine nationalities inhabiting nine different countries (see Figure 3.3). Russians and Ukrainians were the most visible groups (34 per cent and 30 per cent respectively). They were followed by Belarussians (14 per cent) and Armenians (13 per cent). Other nationalities each constituted 2 or 3 per cent of the sample.

With respect to place of residence, two trends were visible. First, respondents from regions located close to the Polish border represented a very large element of the sample, Second, respondents also tended to come from major cities: Moscow, St. Petersburg and Kiev.

For 70 per cent of the respondents, the primary aim of the current trip was to trade, for 15 per cent it was to seek employment. Petty-traders were mainly women, whereas among job-seekers men prevailed significantly. In statistical terms, an analysis of respondents' frequency of visits to Poland showed a strong right-hand asymmetry of distribution, since the average number of visits amounted to 13.35 while the median was 5 and mode 1.

66 *Poland's Post-War Dynamic of Migration*

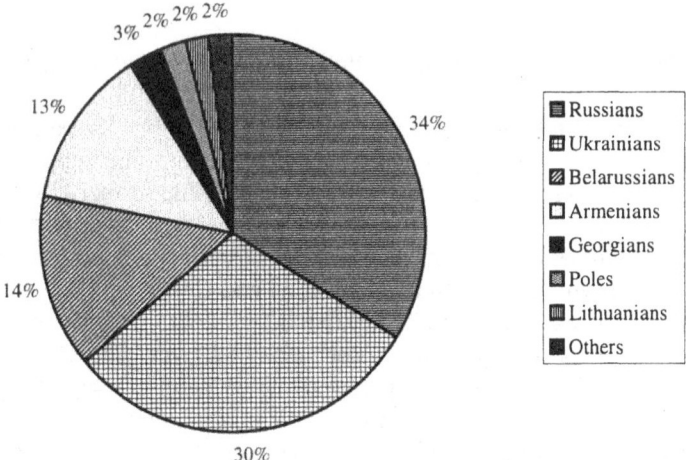

Source: Iglicka, 1999a, p. 128

Figure 3.3 Respondents by nationality

Therefore the strategy employed by former Soviet citizens was characterised by a high frequency of movement, which made the earnings gap between monthly salary and monthly profit (number of trips times profit per trip) even wider (Iglicka, 1999a).

> I am a neuropathologist and love my job, which I do not want to leave. However, my salary is not enough to live on. That is why on Fridays after work I board a coach and, with my bags full of goods, go to Poland. Early on Saturday morning I am already at the bazaar, and by Sunday evening I am back at home. The income is small but allows me to keep my head above water for a while (Khomra, 1994, p. 147).

Some developments in the shuttle mobility strategy were already observable in that 1995 survey. Some respondents who, at the beginning of 1990s, treated petty-trade as a temporary livelihood found regular employment in their home countries (through setting up firms based on the commercial connections in Poland). In some other cases, the strategy of shuttle mobility led to permanent employment in the Polish-Belarussian, Polish-Russian or Polish-Ukrainian black or grey markets.

The results of the survey did not indicate that Poland was perceived by the respondents as a destination area but rather as a very good arena for "learning about being abroad," "conducting and building up businesses" and, perhaps most importantly, "networking," which in the future may let them infiltrate the grey economic zones of Western Europe (Iglicka, 1999a).

As many as 51 per cent of the respondents expressed their intention to work in Western Europe. Here males predominated slightly (see Figure 3.4), whereas females were in majority among the 62 per cent of respondents who wanted to settle abroad (see Figure 3.5).

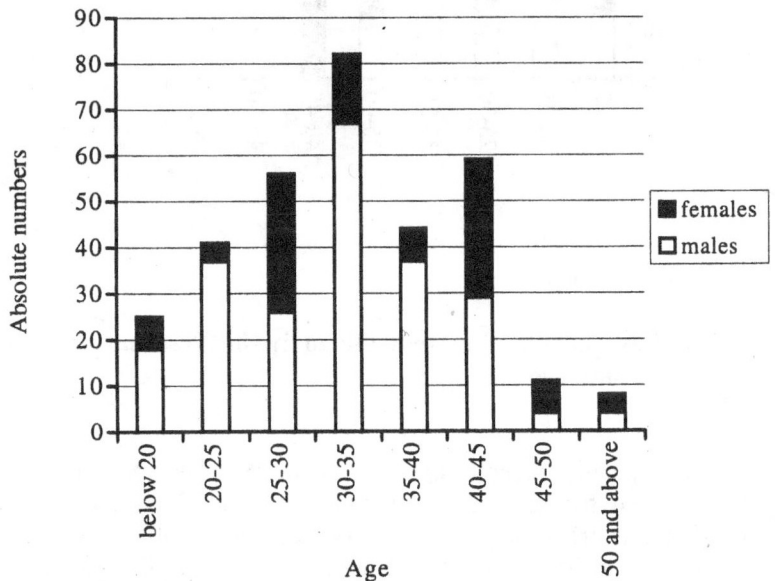

Source: Iglicka, 1999a, p. 138

Figure 3.4 Respondents who would like to work in Western Europe by sex and age

Generally speaking, well-educated respondents preferred to work abroad and less-educated respondents expressed preference to settle there (Iglicka, 1999a). The interdependence between education level and attitudes towards working abroad (i.e. Western Europe) showed a moderate dependence (Cramer coefficient $V = 0.347$) whereas the interdependence between respondents' education and willingness to settle in Western Europe was rather weak ($V = 0.297$).

Another study, conducted by the Center for Migration Studies of Warsaw University in 1996, was based on a much smaller quota-target

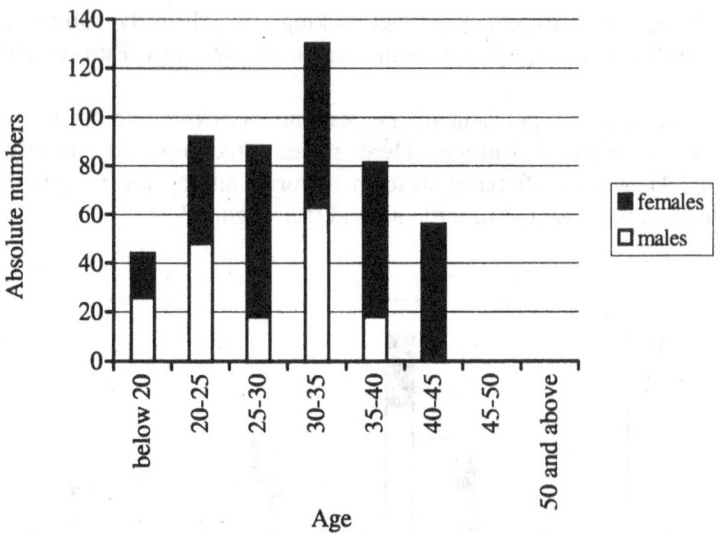

Source: Iglicka, 1999a, p. 139

Figure 3.5 Respondents who would like to live in Western Europe by sex and age

sample of 156 unregistered "migrants" in the Warsaw urban agglomeration.[6] These were foreigners either working in Poland or generating income from conducting trade or providing services without official documents permitting them to do so. Due to the impossibility of carrying out a random sample and a lack of credible data, researchers established the criteria concerning proportions of respondents by origin, sex and activities conducted. It was decided that approximately 80 per cent of the respondents should consist of citizens of the former USSR, women were to comprise 40 per cent and no less than half of the respondents were to be persons working in Poland (Iglicka et al., 1997).

Findings from this survey confirmed some of the results of my previous border survey. Very young (up to 24 years of age) and young people significantly dominated among the respondents. Persons with secondary education prevailed, constituting more than 45 per cent of the sample. More than 80 per cent of the interviewees came from big cities. The most common reason for which respondents came to Poland was "the example set by acquaintances" (40 per cent) and "the opportunity to earn well" (32 per cent).

Table 3.6 Respondents according to reason for coming to Poland (%)

Reason	Respondents
Previous trip(s) to Poland	4.6
Close proximity	19.2
Inexpensive transportation	8.6
Easy to obtain documents	3.9
Following the example set by the others	40.0
Easy to find work	7.9
Possibility of earning well	31.6
Standard of living in Poland	7.9
Poor situation in country of origin	5.9
Other	7.2
Absolute number	156

Source: Iglicka et al., 1997, p. 22

Contrary to the findings from the border survey, more than 20 per cent of the Warsaw interviewees responded that they plan to stay for "more than a year," "as long as possible" or "permanently" in Poland. Many respondents in this survey expressed a desire to work in the West but added that this was not possible because of the difficulties in obtaining visas.

Table 3.7 Respondents according to plans for remaining in Poland (%)

Duration of stay	Respondents
Several days	18.0
1-2 months	9.1
A month or two	11.0
Several months	18.5
Approximately a year	3.1
Several years	3.9
As long as possible	12.0
Permanently	4.2
Hard to say	20.1
Absolute numbers	156

Source: Iglicka et al., 1997, p. 23

This may indicate that some respondents, and especially those with an already existing network and connections in Poland, upon realising the difficulty of migrating into Western Europe, turn to consider the possibility of long-term or permanent settlement to Poland. 'Commerce-driven activity is turning into labour mobility; in other words, those who came initially as traders are familiarising themselves with the terrain, local customs and regulations, and taking the opportunity to settle in Poland as workers. In some cases, this involves 'pendulum traders' settling (either legally or illegally) and acting as agents for other traders – usually fellow-countrymen. However, yet others have been finding employment either on a casual or a regular basis, outside trade (Sword, 1999, p. 164). In the second half of the 1990s, therefore, some part of *primitive mobility* turned slowly into typical migration in the Central European buffer zone.

Notes

1. The Aliens Law is a comprehensive document that regulates: 1) the entry, exit, transit and residence of foreign nationals; 2) activities of the state and various government agencies' scopes of responsibility pertaining to migration; 3) the rights of foreigners, in keeping with international standards; and 4) the repatriation of ethnic Poles (Stachanczyk, 1998; Jagielski, 1997).
2. Citizens of the former USSR (with the exception of Armenians) do not need visas to enter Poland. Agreements on visa-free movements (of up to 90 days) were signed between Poland and Estonia (1993), Poland and Lithuania (1993), Poland and Latvia (1992) and Poland and Ukraine (1997). Other former Soviet Union countries, namely Azerbaijan, Belarus, Georgia, Kazakhstan, Kirgistan, Russia, Tadijikistan and Turkmenistan still benefit from a 1979 Polish-Soviet agreement. According to this agreement, the only requirement to enter Poland is a voucher and a passport (for tourist travels), an invitation from a Polish citizen and a passport (for private travels) or an AB stamp in the passport (for business trips). Up until 1998, counterfeit invitations and vouchers were available for few dollars at kiosks at the eastern border. The new, stricter policy means that the Border Guard Service has started to check the validity of the documents presented and whether the tourists hold the mandatory minimum quota of money (Iglicka, forthcoming a).
3. The estimate for 1995 posited that migrants holding valid work permits constituted only 0.2 per cent of that figure (Okolski, 1998c).
4. Official annual police registers indicate that the number of crimes committed by foreigners in relation to the total number of foreigners entering Poland is rather low. Police registers record approximately 20,000 judicial proceedings concerning crimes committed by foreigners yearly. The reason is simple: someone living illegally, working illegally and/or conducting business illegally is not likely to file a report with the police if he/she is robbed.
5. The sample number constituted 0.1 per cent of the total number of border crossings from the former USSR at Terespol and Medyka in June and July 1995. The sample was representative for the total population crossing eastern frontier at those places and during that period (for details see Iglicka, 1999a).

6   There were, in fact, three categories of foreigners who were studied in this project. These were: foreigners with a permanent residence permit (102 respondents), foreigners with a visa with a work permit (102 respondents) and "unregistered" migrants i.e. petty-traders or seasonal workers without any official documents allowing them to work or to trade (156 respondents). Only the third category is discussed in this section.

References

Hamilton, F.E.I. and Iglicka, K. (eds) (2000), *From Homogeneity to Multiculturalism. Minorities Old and New in Poland*, SSEES, University of London, London.
Iglicka, K. (1999a), 'The Economics of the Petty-Trade on the Eastern Polish Border' in K. Iglicka and K. Sword (eds), 1999 *The Challenge of East-West Migration for Poland*, Macmillan, St. Martin's, London, New York.
Iglicka, K. (1999b), 'Nomads and Rangers of Central and Eastern Europe', *ISS Working Papers*, no. 32, Warsaw.
Iglicka, K. (2000b), 'Immigrants in Poland – Patterns of Flow', in F.E.I. Hamilton and K. Iglicka (eds), *From Homogeneity to Multiculturalism: Minorities Old and New in Poland*, SSEES, University of London, London.
Iglicka, K. (forthcoming a), 'Migration From and Into Poland in the Light of East-West European Migration', *International Migration*.
Iglicka, K., Jazwinska, E., Kepinska, E. and Korys, P. (1997), 'Imigranci w Polsce w swietle badania etnosondazowego' (Immigrants in Poland in the light of ethnosurvey), *Working Paper*, no. 10, ISS UW, Warsaw.
Iglicka, K. and Sword, K. (eds) (1999), *The Challenge of East-West Migration for Poland*, Macmillan, St. Martin's, London, New York.
Informal Labor Market (1995), *Ministry of Labor Press*, Warsaw.
Jagielski, J. (1997), *Status prawny cudzoziemca w Polsce* (Legal status of foreigners in Poland), Warsaw.
Khomra, A. (1994), *'Torgova migratsiya ukrainskovo naselennyja v Polshu'* (Petty-trade migration of Ukrainian population to Poland), NISS report (typescript), Kiev.
Korcelli, P. (1991),'International Migrations in Europe: Polish Perspectives for the 1990s', *International Migration Review*, vol. 24, no. 2, pp. 1671-89.
Kozlowski, T.K. (1999), 'Migration Flows in the 1990s: Challenges for Entry, Asylum and integration Policy in Poland', in K. Iglicka and K. Sword (eds), *The Challenge of East-West Migration for Poland*, Macmillan, London.
Massey, D.S., et al. (1993), 'Theories of International Migration: Review and Appraisal', *Population and Development Review*, vol. 19, no. 3, pp. 431-65.
Morokvasic, M., and de Tinguy, A. (1993), 'Between East and West: A New Migratory Space', in H. Rudolph and M. Morokvasic (eds), *Bridging States and Markets: International Migration in the early 1990s*, Sigma, Berlin.
Okolski, M. (1996), *Trends in International Migrations. Poland: the 1996 SOPEMI Report*, OECD, Paris.
Okolski, M. (1998c), *Recent trends in international migration – Poland 1998*, SOPEMI report, Paris.
Okolski, M. (1999), 'Recent Migration in Poland: Trends and Causes', in K. Iglicka and K. Sword (eds), *The Challenge of East-West Migration for Poland*, Macmillan, St. Martin's, London, New York.
Petersen, W. (1966), 'A General Typology of Migration', in C.J. Jansen (ed) *Readings in the Sociology of Migration*, Pergamon Press, Oxford.

Poland – *statistical data on migration 1994-1998* (1999), Office for Migration and Refugees, Warsaw.
Polish Border Guard statistics, various years. Warsaw.
Ruch graniczny i wydatki cudzoziemcow w Polsce, 1994-1996 (1997), GUS (Central Statistical Office), Warsaw.
Salt, J. (1996), 'Current trends in international migration in Europe' Council of Europe (paper presented at the 6th Conference of European Ministers responsible for migration affairs), Strasbourg.
Stachanczyk, P. (1998), *Cudzoziemcy. Praktyczny przewodnik do ustawy o cudzoziemcach*, (Foreigners. A practical guide for an Alien Law), Warsaw.
Stola, D. (2000), 'New Migrations to Poland: Conditions and Mechanisms of Development', in F.E.I. Hamilton and K. Iglicka (eds), *From Homogeneity to Multiculturalism: Minorities Old and New in Poland*, SSEES, University of London, London.
Stola, D. (forthcoming), 'Migrations in Central Europe: Poland', in C. Wallace and D. Stola (eds), *Central Europe. The New Migration Space*, Macmillan, London.
Sword, K. (1999), 'Cross-Border "Suitcase Trade" and the role of Foreigners in Polish Informal Markets', in K. Iglicka and K. Sword (eds), *The Challenge of East-West Migration for Poland*, Macmillan, London.
Wallace, C. and Stola, D. (eds) (forthcoming), *Central Europe: The New Migration Space*, Macmillan, London.

4 Patterns of Immigration

Definition, Statistics and the Scope of the Phenomenon

Barring a few exceptions, immigration as recorded by official Polish sources displayed an astonishingly stable pattern in the post-war period – annual inflows ranged from 1,500 to 3,000 (Okolski, 1998c). The sudden increase in the flux of foreigners occurred only after the collapse of the system; inflow from the East and Polish migrants returning from western countries were mainly responsible for this growth (see Figure 4.1 and Table 4.1).

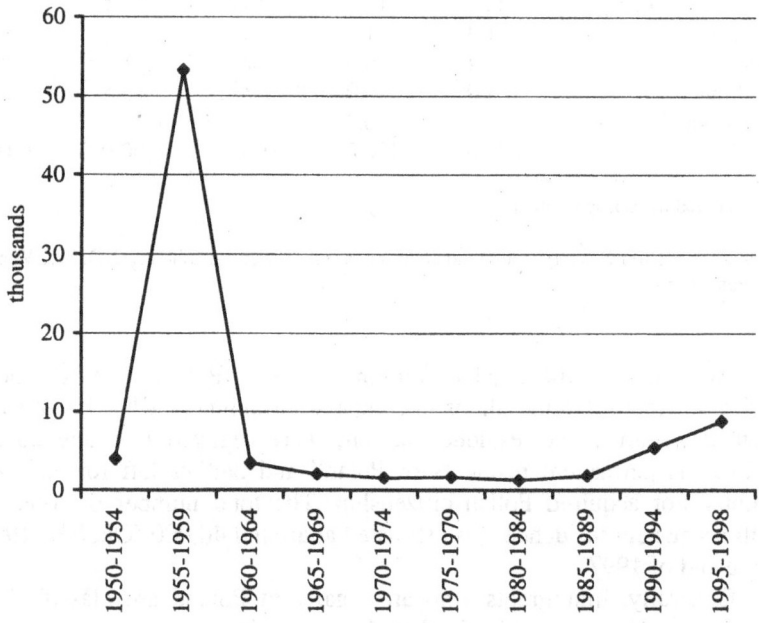

Source: Central Statistical Office

Figure 4.1 Flow of immigrants, 1950-1998

Table 4.1 Immigration to Poland, by country or continent of origin, 1988-1992 (%)

Country/continent	1988	1989	1990	1991	1992
Europe	48.7	42.4	50.3	48.0	49.3
– Austria	2.6	1.3	2.2	3.1	3.0
– Bulgaria	3.6	2.4	1.9	2.4	1.7
– France	4.8	3.9	4.2	3.4	4.3
– Germany	12.7	15.0	22.2	22.2	22.0
– Italy	(a)	(a)	(a)	2.2	2.0
– Sweden	(a)	(a)	(a)	2.4	2.4
– United Kingdom	6.2	4.9	3.7	3.6	4.4
– Other	18.8	14.9	15.7	8.7	9.6
USSR	12.5	11.0	13.9	18.0	16.7
Africa	3.1	2.9	3.3	3.2	2.6
North America	27.3	21.8	21.4	19.5	21.8
– Canada	3.1	3.2	4.3	3.7	4.7
– United States	22.9	16.6	15.0	14.1	15.8
– Other	1.3	1.9	2.2	1.6	1.3
Asia	4.4	6.8	7.7	8.0	6.4
Australia	4.0	3.0	3.3	3.5	3.1
Unknown	–	0.2	–	–	–
Total	100.0	100.0	100.0	100.0	100.0

(a) Included in 'Europe', other

Source: Roczniki Statystyczne (Statistical Yearbooks), Central Statistical Office, Warsaw, various years

According to the legal definition in use in Poland, the statistically registered total of legal aliens encompasses foreigners who, having been granted a permanent residence permit, were registered at any specific address as permanent residents of Poland and neither left for any other country nor acquired Polish citizenship. The total number of foreigners with permanent residence was estimated at around 40,000 (Okolski, 1998c) at the end of 1997.

Generally, immigrants who are legally in Poland are classified and recorded in the respective official statistical registry as:

- Persons granted a permanent residence permit (PRP) – people who have been granted permission to reside and settle in Poland,
- Persons with a right to be legally employed by a Polish employer – people who have received permission to reside in Poland (represented

by what is, in effect, a combined visa-work permit) that must be granted before crossing the Polish border. This visa is granted abròad by a Polish consulate when documents are presented to confirm that the future Polish employer has permission from a specific voivodship labour office to employ the foreigner,
- Persons granted permission to reside in Poland for a prescribed period – people who can present justifiable reasons for residing in Poland. Such reasons are: a) employment explicitly permitted by the authorities; b) economic activities; c) studies; d) marriage to a Polish citizen or to a foreigner who has permanent residence status (some people on this register are also included in the second category and register),
- Persons who have come from abroad to reside permanently and "registered" for permanent residence after arriving in Poland. According to unpublished estimates by the Central Statistical Office, approximately half of those registering for permanent residence in Poland have Polish citizenship (there is overlap between this category and register and the first category and register) (Glabicka and Sakson, 1996).

As there has been no systematic data collection on foreigners in Poland, the data that do exist are scattered among many institutions and, to complicate matters further, some of the above listed registers cover the same individuals. As a result, it is very difficult to establish a proper tally of the foreign population legally staying in Poland. Again, according to the same source (Okolski, 1998c), the foreign population was roughly estimated at least 70,000 at the end of 1997. Recent arrivals from Ukraine, Russia, Belarus and Vietnam account for more than a half of this number.

Channelling the Flux – from *Primitive Mobility* to Migration from the East

It is not possible to prove that people applying for legal immigrant status in Poland are solely the people who started arriving as petty-traders. However, the mass character of *primitive mobility* provokes speculation that many of them did. It is especially true in cases of those with an already-established trade or employment network in Poland who, having come to terms with restrictions in West European policy towards mobility from the "East," started to consider the possibility of long-term or permanent settlement in Poland.[1] There are various ways of legalising one's immigration. The most frequent in official statistics are: application for a permanent residence permit, application for a combined visa-work permit, marriage to a Polish citizen and application for a repatriation visa.[2] Official statistical data indicate an increasing trend of people from the former USSR applying for either a work permit or a permanent residence permit (PRP).

Table 4.2 Visas with work permit granted in 1994-1998 by most numerous nationalities (%)

Country	1994	1995	1996	1997	1998
Ukraine	13.0	14.0	15.8	15.2	13.1
Vietnam	11.0	13.0	14.6	17.8	15.1
Russia	8.5	7.5	7.6	6.5	5.6
USA	7.0	7.0	6.0	5.3	4.1
China	7.8	7.0	7.8	6.5	6.7
Great Britain	7.0	7.0	6.0	5.0	5.0
Belarus	5.0	3.5	3.0	3.3	4.0
Germany	4.6	5.0	6.0	6.0	5.5
Total (absolute numbers)	8690	9057	7019	8978	10505

Source: Poland – statistical data on migration 1994-1998, Office for Migration and Refugees, Warsaw 1999

Table 4.3a Foreigners granted the permanent residence permit (PRP) in Poland according to the most numerous nationalities, 1993-1997** (%)

Country	1993	1994	1995	1996	1997
Ukraine	15	21	19	22	23
Russia	11	12	11	10	8
Belarus	7	6	7	7	8
Germany	5	5	6	5	4
Vietnam	4	4	7	9	8
Kazakhstan*	1	2	8	8	15
Lithuania	3	3	2	3	2
Armenia	1	2	2	2	2
Total (absolute numbers)	1964	2457	3051	2844	4056

* Ethnic Poles and their family members migrating to Poland on the basis of repatriation resolution issued by Polish government in Summer 1996. It is estimated that at least 100,000 ethnic Poles (able to prove ethnic descent) are in Kazakhstan without ever having planned to be there. They (or their predecessors) had been deported to this region by the Soviet (or Tsarist) authorities and could not (or would not) return or move to Poland. The Polish government's resolution on repatriation states that 'persons who can prove Polish origin and are officially invited by local governments in Poland will receive a repatriation visa and

permanent resident status. Immediately upon arrival they will be issued Polish citizenship'. Along with the ethnic Poles arrive their family members who are in a majority not of a Polish descent. So far the repatriation process is regulated by local housing or employment situation but this phenomenon may undoubtedly generate pressure of 'family reunion' oriented migration from the East in the future (Iglicka, 1998c).

** Since 1 January 1998, the former category 'permanent residence permit' has been replaced by two categories: 'permission for settlement' and 'fixed-time residence permit' (for detailed statistics see Table 4.3b)

Source: Poland – Statistical Data on Migration 1994-1998, Office for Migration and Refugees, Warsaw 1999

Table 4.3b Foreigners granted the permanent residence permit (PRP) in Poland according to the most numerous nationalities, 1998-1999 (%)

Country	1998				1999 (a)			
	Permission for Settlement		Permission for fixed-time residence		Permission for Settlement		Permission for fixed-time residence	
	Applications	Granted (b)	Applications	Granted	Applications	Granted	Applications	Granted
Ukraine	16	19	16	18	12	15	14	13
Russia	12	9	8	8	17	19	5	6
Belarus	5	6	5	5	3	1	4	4
Germany	3	3	3	4	0.3	5	5	3
Vietnam	10	8	16	15	9	13	6	10
Kazakhstan (c)	8	–	2	1	-	0.1	2	2
Lithuania	2	2	0.1	1	0.1	0.1	0.1	0.1
Armenia	4	2	8	9	10	7	3	3
Total (absolute numbers)	756	290	9,032	4,849	182	256	7,421	8,880

a) Until 30 June
b) The number of permission granted in a given year may exceed the number of applications submitted in that year because the former also pertains to the applications submitted in previous year
c) Since 1998 ethnic Poles arriving on the basis of repatriation resolution do not need to apply for a PRP. They apply for a repatriation visa only and after arrival to Poland are granted citizenship automatically

Source: Department for Migration and Refugee Affairs, Ministry of Interior and Administration

"For the average European observer, the ratio between positive and negative decisions on PRP applications issued in Poland may seem rather peculiar. Typically, immigration policies in West European countries lead to far more negative decisions issued than positive ones." (Kozlowski, 1999, p. 61).

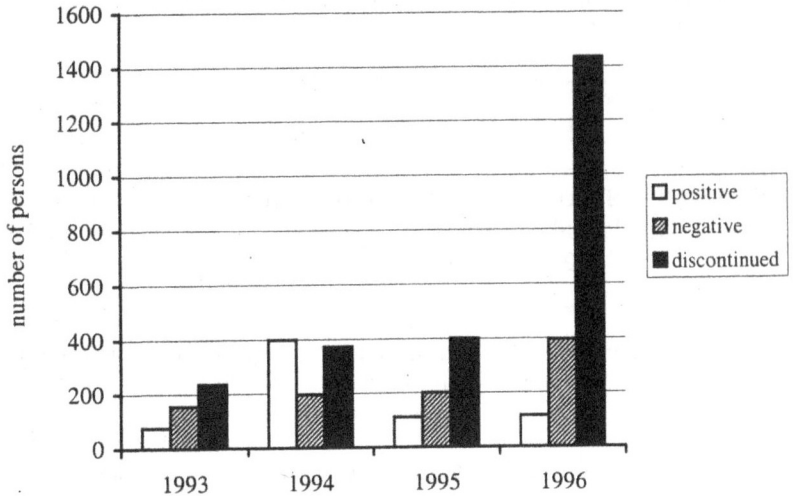

Source: Office for Migration and Refugees data

Figure 4.2 Decisions on permanent residence permit (PRP) in Poland in the period 1993-1996 taken at the first instance

There are a few reasons for this opposite (relative to Western Europe) ratio, but the most important seems to be the extremely decentralised and liberal system of granting PRPs. Some local authorities are far more restrictive or liberal than others are, however a negative decision by one voivodship labour office does not preclude application at another office.

At this point, it is important to note that each year the majority of those recently granted a PRP had either a secondary education (41 per cent) or university education (31.7 per cent). The percentage of people with only a primary education or with a (non-secondary) vocational education fluctuates at only around 11 per cent (Glabicka and Sakson, 1996).

In terms of numbers of combined visa-work permits granted from the beginning of the 1990s till 1996, Ukrainians were in first place, but have since slipped to second. If we look at the nationality of all foreigners granted a permanent residence permit, we see that Ukrainians have remained undoubtedly the most numerous.

What is behind so many Ukrainians, as opposed to citizens of former Soviet countries, such as Belarus, Russia and Lithuania, deciding to immigrate into Poland? This author believes that it is, to some extent, the presence of an ethnic Ukrainian community of approximately 250,000 people, the second (after Germans) largest ethnic group in Poland. Therefore, let me start with a small digression about the historical basis for relations between Poles and Ukrainians in Poland.

It may be surprising for western readers that it is not the Polish-German but the Polish-Ukrainian relationship in which mutual resentments and stereotypes reaching as far back as the 19th century echo loudest (Jedlicki, 1999, p. 228). The most tragic episode began in 1943 when the Ukrainian national guerrilla movement (UPA) started ethnically cleansing Volhynia and eastern Galicia. Reciprocal slaughters and the burning of whole villages were perpetrated (Jedlicki, 1999). The final chapter of the tragic Polish-Ukrainians relations occurred in 1947 when Polish security forces, unable to wipe out the UPA, dislocated approximately 150,000 Ukrainians and Lemkos at gun point from south-eastern Poland (an area which was ethnically Ukrainian) to the northern and western territories (formerly part of Germany). This operation was named Akcja Wisla (Operation Vistula). The events of the Second World War and the post-war period of forced migration have had a significant impact on the Ukrainian minority in Poland during the past 50 years (Babinski, 2000).

The Ukrainians who were forcibly resettled as a result of Akcja Wisla were virtually all relocated to agricultural areas on both vacant individual and state farms. Over the next ten years, some of them found themselves under house arrest and as a group they had no right either to return to their homeland or to travel outside the area in which they lived. This meant they were unable to get an education, a better job or improve their social status.

The Ukrainians were enfranchised with the same rights as Poles only with the end of the Stalinist period in 1956 and, though there were many hurdles to overcome, they did get permission to return to their homeland (Ukraine). Those who decided to stay could also move about, relatively freely, both spatially and socially.

The main changes in Ukrainians' social and political situations happened after 1989. Firstly, their institutions started to flourish. After 1989 the legal status of the Greek Catholic and Orthodox Churches underwent very profound changes and, in fact, one may even say that there has been a real renaissance of these churches in Poland (Babinski, 2000; Iglicka, 2000b).

Poles and Ukrainians now live together and are now generally mixed, both geographically and socially, without any serious conflicts or tensions. This is evident, above all, in the number of ethnically mixed marriages. However, deep under the surface, the events of 1939-1947 are still indelibly imprinted in attitudes toward one another. Fortunately, the mutual resentments present no direct danger or political threat today. Their potential is limited to noisy battles for and against symbolic values, since there is a political will to co-operate on both sides (Jedlicki, 1999, p. 29). The other factor supporting a rather peaceful coexistence of Poles and Ukrainians in Poland is the enormous influx of people from the former USSR into Poland that has been going on since 1989, of which Ukrainians, along with Russians, represent the most important element.

A study on the spatial distribution of foreign-born Ukrainians who held a PRP in 1991 show that they lived in big cities, in ethnically Ukrainian regions and the territories from which Ukrainians and Lemkos were resettled in 1947. Thus, some links between the old Ukrainian diaspora living in Poland for centuries and new arrivals are evident. Furthermore, the territorial distribution of Orthodox and Greek Catholic churches covers the spatial distribution of "new" Ukrainians. It proves that the network between the "old" and "new" group is playing an important role in the geographic circumstances of the latter (Jerczynski, 1999).

Mixed marriages are another interesting phenomenon. It is well known argument that the concluding of marital union with a native person may facilitate integration of a migrant in the host society or help in removing barriers to her/his regularisation. It might be hypothesised that from the Polish perspective until early 1990s mixed marriages frequently and above all served as a vehicle for emigration of Polish citizens while since early 1990s for immigration of foreigners.

In situation of a relatively less tolerant attitude of the authorities in Poland towards irregular foreigners, mixed marriages have become an important means facilitating legalisation of foreigner's stay. It is not possible to state what percentage, if any, of these marriages is fraudulent, but the surge may suggest that there may be some other factors (than traditional) shaping the sudden readiness of Ukrainians (and other nationalities from the former USSR) to marry Poles.[3]

So far, there has been no in-depth, sociological studies on the "new" Ukrainians community. The partial information that exists portrays dynamic, young and very young people, who are rather not (so far) interested in maintaining their ethnic identity while trying to settle in Poland. The "survival strategy" seems to be most important for them. Furthermore, the "new" Ukrainian group is not homogenous and that strategy takes many forms. It is possible however, to distinguish some basic types.

Table 4.4 Total marriages contracted according to the spouses' nationality. Poland: 1990-1998

Year	Total marriages contracted	Both spouses national	Both spouses Foreigners (a)	Mixed marriages Foreign husband	Mixed marriages Foreign wife
1990	255,369	251,129	–	3,329	911
1991	233,206	229,277	–	3,124	911
1992	217,240	213,876	–	2,588	776
1993	207,674	204,597	–	2,323	754
1994	207,689	204,392	–	2,366	931
1995	207,081	203,775	–	2,353	953
1996	203,641	200,411	38	2,177	977
1997	204,850	201,441	37	2,206	1,166
1998	209,378	205,374	35	2,428	1,541

Source: Roczniki Statystyczne (Statistical Yearbooks), Central Statistical Office, GUS, Warsaw, various years

Firstly, those who are in Poland illegally as seasonal workers or petty-traders with the aim to earn quick money and return home, will pursue the shuttle mobility strategy for as long as it will be profitable and as long as the visa-free regime will be in effect. Here, I predict a decrease in petty-traders (which, in fact, has already occurred) and an increase of seasonal workers. Secondly, those who want to settle legally will try to integrate with the Polish majority. They perceive Poland as a country of opportunities and do not want to be associated with the negative stereotypes of being *Soviet*. With the further development of formal and informal networks and institutions, the numbers of Ukrainians granted combined visa-work permits and PRP may be expected to grow.

There is, however, an element in this group that treats Poland only as a stopover on the way to the West. On should also remember a very important fact that, unlike Lithuanians, Belarussians or Russians, quite large Ukrainian ethnic groups are present in Western Europe, the United States and Canada. The ethnic network that undoubtedly assists in the settlement processes of the "new" Ukrainians in Poland would work in other countries as well. Therefore we may assume a third strategy: to obtain Polish citizenship (through naturalisation or marriage) in order to emigrate to the West.

Another interesting migratory phenomenon is that of arrivals from Armenia. This flow is a result of the armed conflict and civil and economic

Table 4.5 Mixed marriages, 1990-1998 (selected years)

Foreign Wife	1990	1995	1996	1997	1998	Foreign husband	1990	1995	1996	1997	1998
Ukraine	–	331	340	456	537	Ukraine	–	89	108	106	119
Russia	–	119	151	127	142	Russia	–	51	38	38	46
Belarus	–	95	104	122	124	Belarus	–	18	21	26	35
Lithuania	–	41	40	33	41	Lithuania	–	8	15	15	15
Armenia	–	27	28	42	53	Armenia	–	44	64	75	140
Latvia	–	6	10	9	10	Latvia	–	–	–	–	–
Kazakhstan	–	13	11	10	23	Kazakhstan	–	–	–	–	–
USSR	255	–	–	–	–	USSR	210	–	–	–	–
Germany	370	61	63	53	74	Germany	1494	748	698	649	632
Vietnam	–	15	42	110	310	Vietnam	–	45	79	152	251
USA	88	46	33	39	22	USA	263	185	138	126	99
United Kingdom	14	–	–	–	–	United Kingdom	44	100	92	98	124
Canada	–	17	15	7	15	Canada	0	46	43	30	46
Others	184	149	140	–	–	Others *	1318	986	881	891	921
Total	911	920	977	1166	1541	Total	3329	2320	2177	2206	2428

* Mainly Western European countries

Source: Roczniki Statystyczne (Statistical Yearbooks), Central Statistical Office, GUS, Warsaw, various years

strife in the Caucasuses; therefore, Armenians arrive in Poland mainly as political refugees. Contrary to other asylum seekers in Poland, they do not treat Poland exclusively as a country of transit to the West. As far as the applications for asylum are concerned, Armenians are the only nationality figuring for the whole 1992-1998 period. Other nations (with the exception of former Yugoslavia) reflect mainly the "popularity" of Poland as a way to Western Europe (see Figure 4.3).

> All countries of central and eastern Europe, including the CIS, are experiencing another, heretofore almost unknown, migration stream, namely irregular and illegal transit migration. Many migrants are coming to these countries not to settle down or work temporarily, but intending to move on further to the west. The countries of central and eastern Europe and the CIS have become a significant route for migrants from the third world (Frejka, 1996, p. 7).

The majority of asylum seekers in Poland consist of people who were detained on either the eastern or western border, elsewhere in the country or after having been deported from Germany. "Given the increasingly limited opportunities to migrate to Western European countries legally, it is widely believed that an increasing proportion of migrants who are heading for the West through the CEEs use the services of smugglers for at least some part of their journey. There is also concern that the emerging asylum system in the CEEs is being abused by smugglers who advise migrants to claim asylum when smuggling operations breakdown" (Migration in Central and Eastern Europe, 1999, p. 41). The statistical formulation of this phenomenon is illustrated in Figure 4.4, which shows the relations between types of decisions on asylum claims made in Poland between 1993 and 1998. Most important here are not the numbers themselves but the highly disproportionate number of decisions to discontinue asylum claims versus other decisions. The decisions on discontinuance means that the refugee status claimants had disappeared; as we can see from the below they do indeed vanish (Kozlowski, 1999).

To return to those among asylum seekers who are most likely to want to stay in Poland for at least a few years, i.e. Armenians, some of them view application for a permanent residence permit to be the best way to achieve legal Polish residence, while others see it to be marriage with a Polish citizen. The majority of them still think about going back home and therefore seem to prefer irregular status (i.e. extended visas). Yet others stay illegally.

84 *Poland's Post-War Dynamic of Migration*

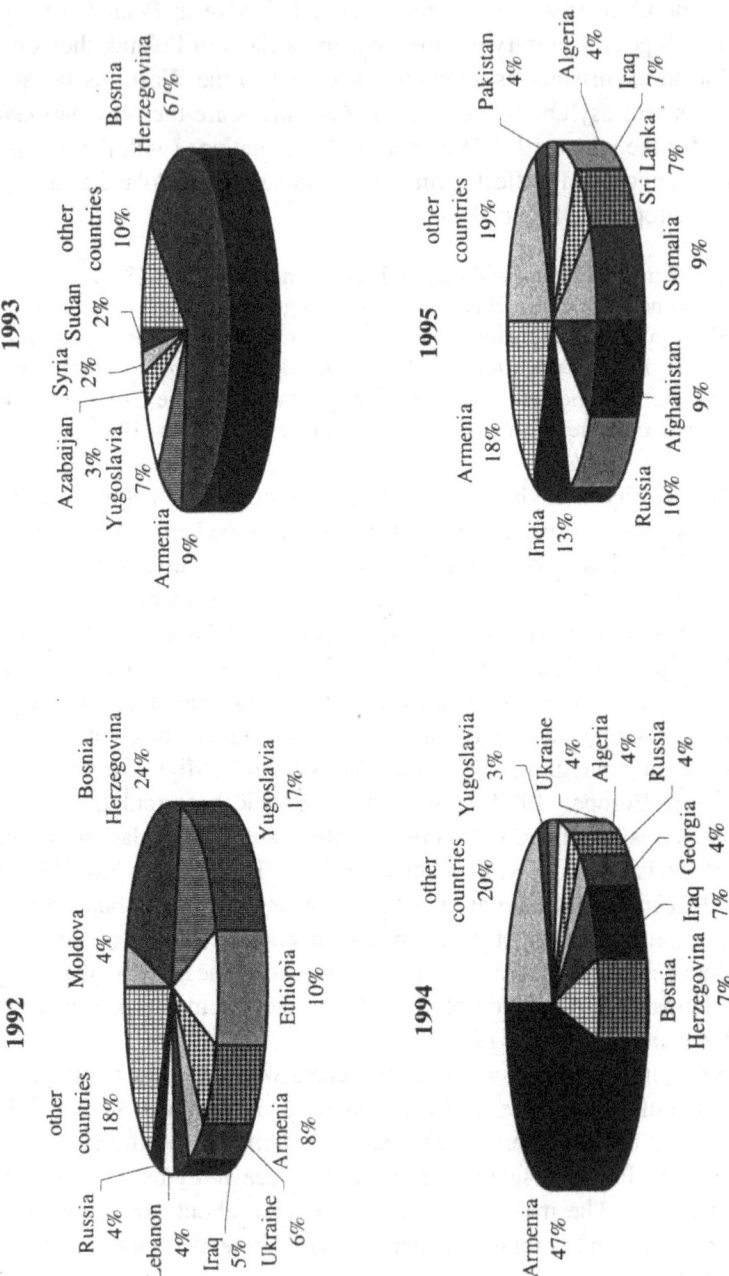

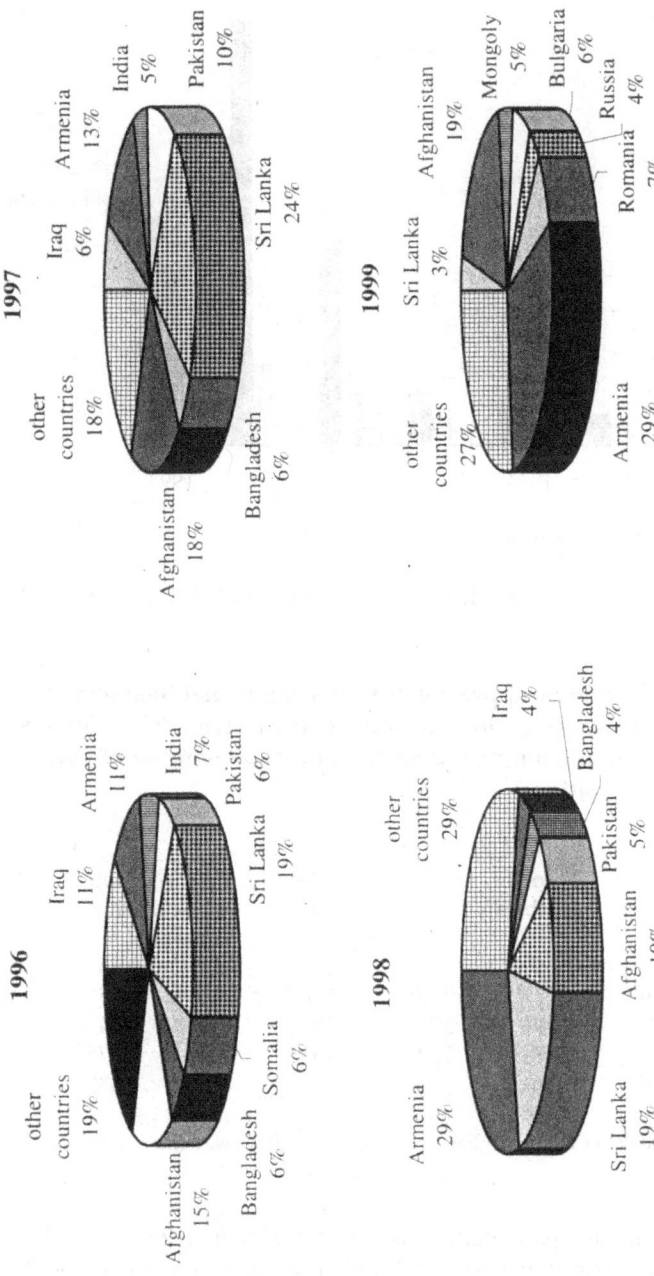

Source: Office for Migration and Refugees data

Figure 4.3 Asylum seekers by main countries of citizenship (including accompanying family members), 1992-1999

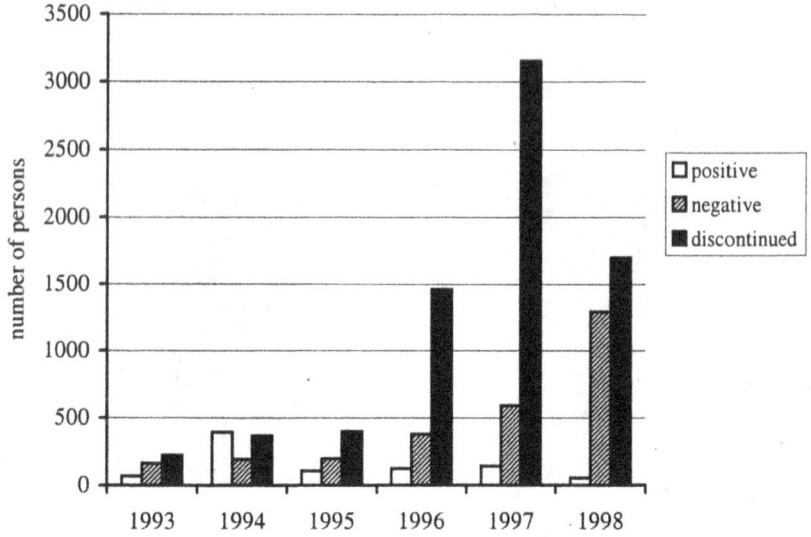

Source: Office for Migration and Refugees data

Figure 4.4 Decisions on refugee claims in Poland, 1993-1998

Table 4.6 Cases of disappearance or leaving the national territory during the asylum procedure in selected CEEs, 1995-1997 (absolute numbers and % of the total number of asylum applications)

Country	1995		1996		1997	
	Absolute numbers	%	Absolute numbers	%	Absolute numbers	%
Bulgaria	–	–	122	40.0	87	21.0
Czech Republic	517	37.0	678	31.0	839	40.0
Poland	394	57.0	1,457	45.0	3,148	89.0
Romania	155	22.0	93	16.0	75	5.0
Slovak Republic	–	–	–	–	539	84.0

Source: Migration in Central and Eastern Europe, 1999 Review, Geneva, IOM, p. 134

Armenians are particularly visible in trade, frequently illegal, street market trade. Armenians have created their own micro-communities in Northern and Eastern Poland. Along with their arrival came a slow ethnic reawakening among the small, centuries-old group of "old" Armenians in Poland that has been almost totally assimilated.

Researchers have noted that most new arrivals are well-educated people (Marciniak, 2000). Rarely, however, do they find employment commensurate with their knowledge and skills.

As already mentioned, immigration to Poland from the early 1960s to the beginning of the 1990s was not statistically significant. However, one of the existing and quite visible inflows was the movement of Vietnamese students – who arrived in Poland as part of either a government-sponsored programme of "socialist co-operation" or academic exchange. After graduation, most of them returned home, where having a European diploma distinguished them in the Vietnamese social hierarchy.

Since 1989, though still a communist country, Vietnam has started to pursue a more liberal migration policy that led to outflows to Poland, not only of students (mostly from privileged families), but also of people looking for somewhere to work and live.

Since the end of 1993, the number of Vietnamese citizens applying for work permit-visas has seen a sharp increase, and there has been a corresponding rise in the number of Vietnamese legally entering Poland. Vietnamese were the second largest group (after Ukrainians) up until 1996in terms of the number of combined visa-work permits granted (see Table 4.2). Since 1997 they are in first place. Moreover, the growing presence of Vietnamese is also due to illegal flow. Some of these illegals have attempted to legalise their stay through an application for a permanent residence permit or through marriage with a Polish resident. At the end of 1995, the Vietnamese were the third largest group of immigrants receiving residence permits (see Table 4.3a). In 1996 they were the second, and this tendency has kept up to the present day (mid 1999). An estimated 30,000 Vietnamese live in Poland (Halik, 2000).

Vietnamese have become one of the main groups of foreigners involved in small (as opposed to petty) trade. It is a group that is well organised socially and, contrary to Armenians and Ukrainians, has not been involved much in crime and misdemeanours. There is much to indicate that they feel "at home." They send their children to Polish schools, learn the Polish language, read Polish papers and watch Polish TV. They carry on a lively economic activity, not only in the fields of small trade and gastronomy. They declare a feeling of "well-being" within the Polish cultural sphere and they stress the tolerance and the possibility of being able to have an "economic existence" within it. One should, however, remember that the Vietnamese form a fairly close-knit society which "externally" adapts itself to the dominant culture while "internally" retaining their own linguistic, ethnic and cultural identity (Condominas and Pottier, 1983).

Three possible scenarios of the future development of the Vietnamese community may be proposed after an analysis of official data on Vietnamese society and an examination of the results of research on the cultural awareness of the Vietnamese in Poland (Halik, 1995). First, if the bulk of immigrants are young, poorly educated males who stay in Poland illegally only to earn money, after achieving this goal, they will probably decide to return to Vietnam or try to migrate onward to the West. Such a scenario would mean that, in the foreseeable future, there will either be fewer Vietnamese immigrants in Poland or the number arriving will remain at the same level. The second scenario predicts that the Vietnamese who are in Poland legally, especially those who have permanent residence and who also have network connections with their compatriots in Germany or France, will probably treat their stay in Poland as a "stopover." Thus, while enjoying a "friendly environment" and "an atmosphere of tolerance," they can save up money and wait for Polish citizenship to enter a western European country easily and legally. This again foretells a stabilisation or a slow decrease in numbers. The last scenario has, along with the continued thriving of the Polish economy, a possibility of an increase in the number of Vietnamese permanently residing in Poland, which will gradually lead to their integration.

Survey Results

At this point, it is reasonable to turn to the results of the survey on immigrants in Warsaw agglomeration. In the previously-mentioned 1996 study (see page 68) three categories of immigrants were studied: foreigners with permanent residence permits (PRP), foreigners with visas and unregistered migrants. The third category was already discussed in the section on *primitive mobility* from the East. Here I analyse the two other groups, namely immigrants with a PRP and ones with work visas.

Despite researchers' best efforts, it proved impossible (largely because of the high percentage of cancelled interviews) to obtain statistically-adequate representative samples of the two groups. Unfortunately, the alternative sampling method that had to be used (continued random samplings to replace unrealised interviews) and the differences observed in the list of selected traits between the sample and the population do not qualify the sampling as representative. For these reasons, any further analysis of either sampling should be treated as strictly target samplings.

Men were in a noticeable minority among the 202 respondents (100 with PRP and 102 with visas). A clear predominance of women (57 per cent) was visible especially among immigrants with a PRP. This proportion is rather puzzling in that the official registers indicate a clear predominance of men over women among those granted permanent residence permits. One explanation might be the fact that the most common reason for granting permanent residence permits is marriage to a Polish citizen; hence, it is possible that there was a higher proportion of women with permanent residence permits married to Polish citizens in the sample than there is in the overall foreign population.

In general, the immigrants surveyed were young or very young: respondents under the age of 39 made up 70 per cent of the total surveyed. Immigrants with a PRP were decisively older than respondents with visas were. Almost 20 per cent of the former were aged 60 and more. It seems very likely, therefore, that the first group of respondents included a group of Polish return migrants who, after spending years abroad, decided to spend their retirement back in Poland.

Married migrants comprised close to 60 per cent while single, non-widowed, non-divorced people made up 32 per cent of the total number of respondents. This feature was observed in both groups, though the difference between married and single immigrants is higher among immigrants with a permanent resident permit. This is not unusual given the decidedly older age structure of this group.

Table 4.7 Structure of two migrant groups according to citizenship (%)

Citizenship	Permanent Residence Permits (PRP)	Visas (temporary residence permits)
Countries of the former USSR	47.0	20.8
Countries of the former Soviet bloc	24.0	9.4
West European Countries	10.0	11.3
USA & Canada	6.0	2.8
Vietnam	3.0	14.2
Other Asian countries	–	22.6
Africa	2.0	9.4
Others, including Stateless persons	8.0	9.4
Absolute number	100	100

Source: Iglicka et al., 1997, p. 16

Citizens of the former USSR formed the majority of immigrants with permanent residence permits (47 per cent) and immigrants with visas

(21 per cent). Western Europeans, Americans and Canadians also stand out (16 per cent) among permanent residence permit holders while Asians make up a surprising 27 per cent of migrants with visas (14 per cent of whom are from Vietnam).

The overwhelming majority of respondents overall (80 per cent) originated from urban areas, and urbanites accounted for 96 percent of migrants with visas (temporary residence permits). This is clearly related to the importance of their level of education. The results of the survey confirm the general trends observed in official statistics on the education of people granted PRPs in Poland. They show that most respondents were well educated or very well educated. Among those with visas, university graduates dominated significantly while respondents with only primary education made up less than 1 per cent. People with a secondary education comprised 42 per cent and 40 per cent of respondents with permanent residence permits were university graduates.

Some interesting facts are brought to light from an analysis of the structure of the two migrant groups by family relations in Poland. Namely, more than 60 per cent of respondents with a permanent residence permit and almost 80 per cent of respondents with a visa did not have any Polish ancestors or relatives in Poland. Of the total sample, 70 per cent of the respondents had no family ties whatsoever. Another 12 per cent were unsure. These numbers might indicate that Poland, as a destination country, was chosen "at random" by many of the respondents of this study. Many more respondents with permanent residence permits have Polish relatives or ancestors (30 per cent) than do respondents with visas (10 per cent).

Table 4.8 Structure of two migrant groups according to family relations in Poland (%)

Polish Ancestry	Permanent Residence Permits (KSP)	Visas (temporary residence permit)
Yes	30.0	10.4
No	64.0	78.3
Do not know	5.0	10.4
No data	1.0	0.9
Absolute numbers	100	102

Source: Iglicka et al., 1997, p. 32

The structure of reasons for which respondents came to Poland is also quite interesting. The most common reason given among all respondents was "the example set by acquaintances." Other important reasons for coming to Poland cited by immigrants with a permanent residence permit were "earlier connections with Poland" and "the standard of living in Poland." Among respondents with visas: "the possibility of earning well," "the standard of living in Poland" and "easy to find work."

As mentioned above, the data included in Table 4.8 suggest that surveyed respondents have chosen Poland as an immigration country more often randomly than deliberately, although data from Table 4.9 shows that some reconnaissance had been made before arrival.

Table 4.9 Structure of two migrant groups according to reason for coming to Poland (%)

Reasons for choosing Poland	Permanent Resident Permits (KSP)	Visas (temporary residence permits)
Previous trip(s) to Poland	18.0	7.5
Close proximity	16.0	2.8
Inexpensive transportation	10.0	2.8
Easy to obtain documents	5.0	1.9
Following the example set by others	24.0	16.0
Easy to find work	7.0	11.3
Possibility of earning well	7.0	16.0
Standard of living in Poland	17.0	11.3
Poor situation in country of origin	3.0	3.8
Other	17.0	22.0
Absolute numbers	100	102

Source: Iglicka et al., 1997, p. 33

Responses regarding plans for remaining in Poland varied considerably. About two-thirds of the immigrants with a permanent residence permit claimed that they want to remain in Poland permanently and another 15 per cent stated that they would like to stay "as long as possible" (see Table 4.10).

It is noteworthy that the predominant response concerning future plans was "it's hard to say" among respondents with visas. The next common answer for this group was "for several years," followed by "for as long as possible." This bears out our previous assumptions concerning survival strategies of legal foreign residents of Poland.

Table 4.10 Structure of two migrant groups according to plans for remaining in Poland (%)

How long will the migrant stay in Poland	Permanent Residence Permits (KSP)	Visas (temporary residence permits)
Several days	1.0	0.9
10-20 months	1.0	–
a month or two	–	1.9
Several months	1.0	11.3
Approx. A year	–	5.6
Several years	4.0	22.6
as long as possible	14.0	12.3
Permanently	61.0	7.5
hard to say	15.0	37.7
No data	2.0	–
Absolute numbers	100	102

Source: Iglicka et al., 1997, p. 35

Formation of Immigrants' Groups

Since 1945, virtually all highly developed Western countries have experienced relatively large-scale immigration. In comparing these countries, Castles and Miller (1993) found the following common characteristics: (i) a dynamic process of migration, which transforms the temporary entry of workers and refugees into permanent settlers who form distinct ethnic groups; (ii) economic and social marginalisation of the immigrants; (iii) community formation among immigrants; (iv) increasing interaction between immigrant groups and the local population; and (v) the imperative for the state to react to immigration and ethnic diversity (Castles, 1995, p. 293). Of course, these represent only the key structural similarities but they made it possible to establish some common patterns despite differences in detail.

Although isolated from these experience for much of the post-war period, post-communist Central European countries are now in the preliminary stage, that is to say of the inflow of foreigners. As yet, it is hard to draw any firm conclusions for this region regarding either immigration features or the reactions of the national government and local communities to this phenomenon. I think, however, that the globalisation of migration will soon involve Central and East European countries in ways that approximate Castles' model (Hamilton and Iglicka, 2000; Iglicka, forthcoming b).

Official statistics and survey findings cited in previous chapters reveal that ethnic groups' formation is already in process in Poland. New and exotic (for this part of Europe) diasporas of Vietnamese, Chinese and Armenians are rapidly aggregating. In the future, they may create "global tribes" with their own ethnic and cultural identity that will not disappear despite distance from their homelands. These tribes are the modern-day equivalent of cosmopolitan nations from the classical era. Their arrival in various spots on the globe has resulted in the transfer and development of new technologies, industry and culture (Kotkin, 1993). Their departure has always resulted in the withering of these spheres. Their arrival has been the harbinger of technological, economic and intellectual advancement and has contributed to the development of the global market place.

A dynamic migratory process is transforming the temporary entry of Armenians, Ukrainians and Vietnamese into settlement in Poland. Although all three groups mean to integrate with Polish society, as yet it is hard to draw any broad conclusions for the prospects of ethnic groups under formation. It must be pointed out that economic performance in general and earnings convergence in particular, determine the degree of assimilation, but the degree of assimilation itself has an impact on performance (Glytsos, 2000). Will immigrants face economic and social marginalisation in Poland? Will there be tension between them and the local population forcing the state to react to growing ethnic diversity? It is too early to answer all these questions as Poland is only at the onset of the process. However, it is important to mention here that Polish law guarantees ethnic minority rights only to Polish citizens.[4] Given the revival of some "old" minorities such as Lithuanians, Ukrainians or Armenians, the appearance of new immigrant minorities such as the "new" Ukrainians, "new" Armenians and Vietnamese, that include non-citizens, the issue of the legal protection of their rights will become important very soon (Michalska, 1997).

Some sociologists argue that the problem of the exclusion of certain groups (among them immigrants) from the mainstream of society is one of the most important social conflicts in advanced societies. It is certainly true in Western European societies, but this author does believe that it is too early to consider the issue of immigrants in the Central Europe from the point of view of the phenomenon of social exclusion.

Since two of the aims of this book are to show that some social and population processes related to the inflows of people reached Poland only after the collapse of the political-economic system, and that Poland – as a latecomer to the global stage – can serve as a model and example of changes in population developments, let us briefly analyse the situation and role of immigrants in Western Europe 20-30 years ago to determine any similarities or differences with the situation of immigrants in modern-day Poland.

Ethnic Division on Emerging Foreign Labour Markets[5]

Conceptual Framework

At the beginning of the 1970s, the conflict between labour and capital was considered one of the most important social issues in immigrant groups' formative process. The problem of labour market segmentation was a key point of the analysis. Labour market segmentation has complex links with other factors that lead to the marginalisation of immigrant groups. "Low-status work, high unemployment, bad working conditions and lack of opportunities for promotion are both causes and results of the other determinants of minority status: legal disabilities, insecure residency status, residential concentration in disadvantaged areas, poor educational prospects and racism" (Castles and Miller, 1993, p. 183).

Economists noted the segmentation of the labour market into primary and secondary sectors, which is a characteristic of advanced industrial economies (Gordon, 1972; Edwards, 1975; Piore 1979; Portes, 1981). In the capital-intensive primary sector, employers invest in workers by providing specialised training and paying for their education. Severance benefits are contractually guaranteed. Jobs, although complicated, are secure, workers are professionals and begin to resemble capital for employers (Piore, 1979).

As far as the foreign labour force is concerned, the primary labour market generally tends to occur through the legal channels; immigrant employees have legal status mainly on the basis of a work-permit and visa or permanent residence. Ethnicity does not play an important role here since workers are hired mainly according to ability. Immigrants tend to have mobility opportunities comparable to those of native workers. They may start at the bottom of the job ladder but work conditions and remuneration match the domestic workforce's. The function of imported employees in the primary sector is usually to supplement the domestic labour force rather than to discipline it (Portes, 1981).

The primary sector in receiving countries is responsible for brain drain in sending countries. Thus, for example, the third and sixth preference categories of the amended 1954 U.S. Immigration Act are reserved for professionals, technical, and skilled workers in short supply there (Portes, 1981, p. 283).

Contrary to the above, the labour-intensive secondary sector recruits workers who do not need prior training, have little or no upward career opportunities and are at the bottom of the wage scale. Low wages, unstable conditions, and the lack of reasonable prospects for promotion in this sector make it difficult to attract native workers. Thus, in modern market economies, there is a permanent demand for workers who are prepared to work in such unfavourable, insecure and unstable conditions (Piore, 1979). Employers turn to immigrants to fill labour supply shortages or wage supply-demand disequilibrium. Therefore immigration flows into this market have characteristics opposite to those absorbed by the primary sector. First of all, immigrants' legal status on this market ranges from illegal to temporary stay only. Legal permanent residence is rare. Ethnicity plays an important role here since workers are hired mainly by ethnicity. Immigrants are hired for short-term jobs (sometimes seasonal only), meaning no opportunities for upward mobility. The main role of immigrants here is to "discipline" the domestic labour force by lowering prevailing wage (Portes, 1981).

> Within receiving societies, once immigrants have been recruited into particular occupations in significant numbers, these jobs become culturally labelled as 'immigrant jobs.' The stigma comes from the presence of immigrants, not from the characteristics of the job. In most European countries, for example, jobs in automobile manufacturing came to be considered 'immigrant jobs', whereas in the United States they are considered 'native jobs' (Massey et al., 1993, p. 453).

In the following sections, changes in population mobility in Poland since the collapse of the communist system and their impact on labour markets are discussed. Two flows of migration into Poland are distinguished: the one from its East and the one from the West and their impact on Poland's primary and secondary labour markets. It is assumed that the formation of a foreign labour force or immigrant enclave on the labour market "is not a product of deliberate economic policies by the state or labour needs of the capitalist class, but depends on the initiative and resources of the immigrants themselves. Their emergence is contingent, however, on a series of unique historical circumstances" (Portes, 1981, p. 291).

New population phenomena that followed the fall of the communist system have had an enormous impact on labour markets. The most important were:

- an influx of people from neighbouring countries, particularly the former Soviet Union, arriving as part of visa-free shuttle movements (*primitive mobility*),

- an influx of foreigners who require visas to enter Poland,
- "permanent" immigration (both from the East and from the West).

Labour migration to Poland is a recent phenomenon that gathered momentum only in the 1990s. Moreover, official statistical data indicate that foreigners' access to economic sectors in Poland is segmented according to ethnicity. Movement from the former Soviet Union pertains mainly to the secondary labour market. Asians find employment on both markets, whereas immigrants from the West tend to seek jobs on the primary labour market only. I will elaborate on this thesis in the sections on labour migration from the East and from the West respectively.

Flux from the East

A massive influx of people from the former Soviet Union, arriving as a part of *primitive mobility*, has played a very important role in changes on Polish labour markets, especially at the beginning of transition. In fact, the human movement aimed at profiting from differences in exchange rates and price relations between some newly arisen countries of the former Soviet Union and Poland was a forerunner of future changes on labour markets.

People arriving in Poland to shop have created an enormous demand for many textile and leather products and brought a boom in some parts of the small business sector and thereby new jobs. This has been to the extent that petty-traders from the former Soviet Union have been one of the main growth factors for employment in some parts of Poland's private sector. The huge sums they have spent alleviate somewhat the country's chronic balance of payments.

Some petty-traders in Poland have been engaged in various, usually very short-term jobs in the grey-sphere of the economy. The Polish Ministry of Labour and Social Policy estimates that the majority of the approximately 150,000 foreigners working illegally each year in Poland come from the former Soviet Union. Men work mainly in construction, forestry and fruit farming. Women work in fruit farming as well, and also are frequently employed as seamstresses and in domestic service.

As far as movement of those with regulated legal status is concerned, since 1990 there has been an increasing influx of non-tourists legally arriving and staying in Poland; since very late 1994 these people (and their employers) have had to comply with regulations set out in the Act of Employment and Counteracting Unemployment of December 14, 1994.[6] Since the beginning of transition, voivodeship Labour Offices have issued 10,000 to 15,000 work permits yearly for foreigners working for employers in Poland (Glabicka and Sakson, 1996). During the 1990-1998 period, a total of 80,127 work permits were issued, 63 per cent of which were individual permits and 27 per cent of which were issued for export services and accepted job-contracts. People from the former Soviet Union dominate here significantly (see Table 4.2). Eastern Europeans work mostly as unskilled manual workers, skilled manual workers and artists. Thus even those with work permits occupy, so far, mainly the secondary sector of the labour market; nonetheless, they definitely fill some gaps in local labour markets' supply of workers (see Table 4.11).

Table 4.11 **Work permits for foreigners from Eastern Europe*** according to type of work, 1994 and 1995 (%)

Region	Eastern European Countries		Total	
Year	1994	1995	1994	1995
All management function	25.0	18.5	1651	2024
Owners	33.0	36.0	633	643
Experts specialist and consultant	50.5	40.1	792	698
Administrative personnel	51.7	45.0	224	68
Medical professions	89.5	42.4	68	115
Teachers trainers	43.2	56.5	532	580
Artists	98.1	98.5	666	542
Skilled manual workers	95.8	73.3	573	65
Unskilled manual workers	99.8	62.5	1816	43
Other	82.4	88.0	177	170

* former Soviet Union mainly

Source: Sprawozdanie z badania sondazowego zezwolenia na prace udzielane cudzoziemcom przez wojewodzkie urzedy pracy w okresie 1994 i 1995, Warsaw, Ministry of Labor Press, 1996

Eastern Europeans are hired mainly in such sectors as: agriculture and forestry, construction, manufacturing and transportation. They are hired most often in state-owned and private firms with wholly Polish capital.

Contrary to Eastern Europeans, nationalities from the Far East, e.g. Vietnamese and Chinese, find employment not only in the secondary labour markets but also in the primary ones. In many cases, this is because they hold top positions in the sectors in which they invest, for example restaurants and trading companies. It seems that a few years in Poland were enough for them to adopt strategies to deal with the labour market disadvantages facing foreigners. They searched for "ethnic niches" in which

98 Poland's Post-War Dynamic of Migration

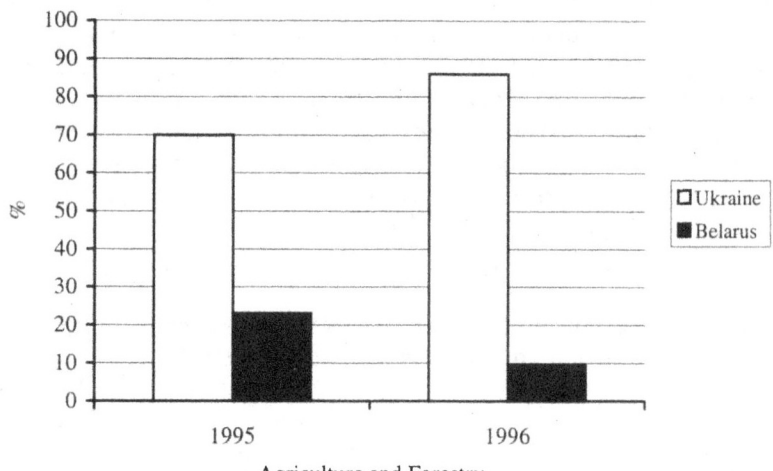

Source: Ministry of Labour Statistics

Figure 4.5a Work permits granted individually by branch of economic activity (main countries of origin) – Agriculture and Forestry, 1995-1996

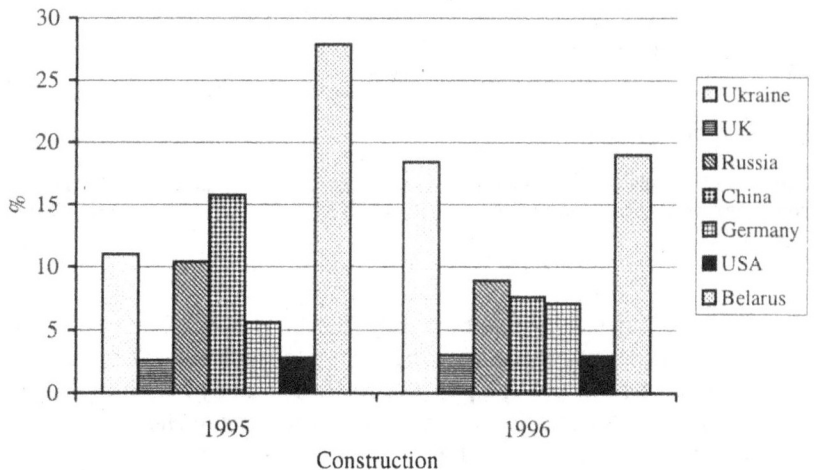

Source: Ministry of Labour Statistics

Figure 4.5b Work permits granted individually by branch of economic activity (main countries of origin) – Construction, 1995-1996

Patterns of Immigration 99

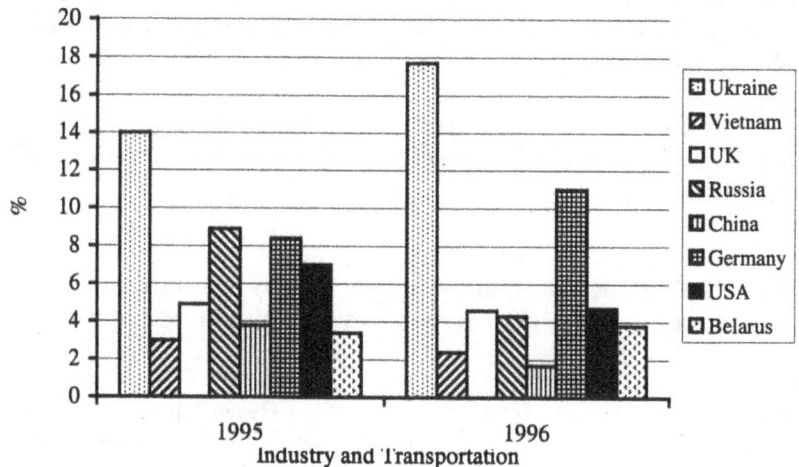

Source: Ministry of Labour Statistics

Figure 4.5c Work permits granted individually by branch of economic activity (main countries of origin) – Industry and Transportation, 1995-1996

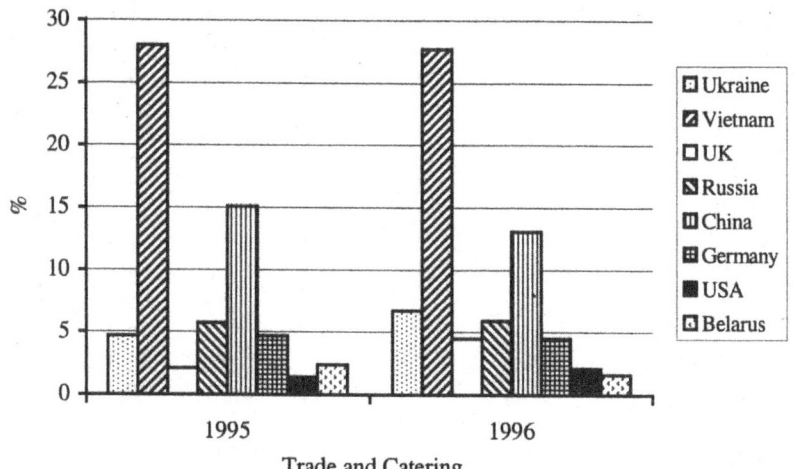

Source: Ministry of Labour Statistics

Figure 4.5d Work permits granted individually by branch of economic activity (main countries of origin) – Trade and Catering, 1995-1996

small business, mutual aid and self-employment were factors conducive to finding low- and high-prestige positions on both primary and secondary markets. They are hired most often in private firms with wholly foreign capital.

Asian nationals are most often employed by food or by trade companies. The trends visible in Table 4.12 and Figure 4.5d remain valid in mid 1999.

Table 4.12 Work permits granted individually by ownership of enterprise (eight top countries of origin) in 1995 and 1996 (%)

Country	Total	State	Private Polish	Private foreign	Private mixed	Other
1995						
Ukraine	17.0	36.6	34.8	1.3	4.7	20.5
Vietnam	10.3	0.6	3.9	22.8	2.6	3.7
United Kingdom	8.5	6.2	9.3	7.4	8.7	13.0
Russia	6.8	11.3	7.6	2.8	11.1	8.2
China	6.5	0.1	1.6	14.4	4.6	0.3
USA	5.5	4.9	3.3	5.8	9.7	6.2
Germany	5.5	7.9	1.4	6.8	10.4	6.5
Belarus	6.4	6.3	14.4	0.8	1.2	10.5
Total (absolute number)	10441	1000	3456	3846	1554	585
1996						
Ukraine	18.7	30.4	39.6	3.1	5.2	27.7
Vietnam	10.2	0.5	4.5	21.1	2.9	2.2
United Kingdom	7.9	5.5	2.1	6.8	9.4	6.3
Germany	6.7	9.5	8.1	7.6	11.9	8.2
Russia	6.1	11.1	6.9	2.9	8.1	5.4
China	5.2	0.5	3.6	11.5	2.2	0.3
USA	5.7	7.4	7.6	5.5	7.0	12.7
Belarus	4.3	8.2	9.8	1.0	2.9	6.1
Total (absolute number)	11915	1133	3741	4657	1771	613

Source: Sprawozdanie z badania sondazowego zezwolenia na prace udzielane cudzoziemcom przez wojewodzkie urzedy pracy w okresie 1995 i 1996, Warsaw, Ministry of Labor Press, 1997

Since 1996, South Koreans are most visible among those Asians who hold executive positions in Poland. In contrast to Chinese and Vietnamese, however, they are employees of large companies. This is connected with the huge investments made by South Korean conglomerates such as Daewoo in Poland.

Flux from the West

Over the past ten years, the movement from the East to Poland has been carefully studied in many research projects (Morokvasic and de Tinguy, 1993; Iglicka and Sword, 1999; Wallace and Stola, forthcoming) whereas the Poland-bound mobility from the West has been almost totally neglected by researchers. Furthermore, statistical data on the phenomena of return migration and mobility from the West are incomplete. Therefore this section is based almost exclusively on the findings from the only survey of its kind, conducted by German researchers from the Wissenschaftszentrums Berlin fur Sozialforschung in 1995 on managerial migration from the West into Poland.[7]

At the outset it is important to note that the influx from the West cannot be compared with that from the East in numerical terms. The numbers are simply much lower. However, the inflow from the West has had a substantial qualitative impact on the recent changes in the Polish economy generally and on labour markets particularly.

The basic finding that stems in this study is that, contrary to the movement from the East, mobility from the West pertains only to the primary labour markets and, moreover, it is a highly institutionalised phenomenon. Westerners find employment mainly in such economic branches as industry and transportation, education and, to some extent, construction (see Figures 4.5b, c, e).

The transfer of skills and know-how from the West is accompanying the transformation of the Polish economy. This process includes human mobility along the West-East axis. The mobility from the West is one of the factors behind the phenomenon of the "brain-gain," (reverse brain drain) visible since 1994 in migratory trends in Poland.

This not only manifests itself in the fact that each year the average education of immigrants granted a PRP is much higher than emigrants' (see Figure 4.6) but also because more immigrants than emigrants occupy managerial or professional posts at the time of registration (Okolski, 1995).

Table 4.13 shows that Western Europeans and North Americans held, for the most part, managerial functions. As well, they were employed quite frequently as experts, specialists and consultants.

They were granted work permits in enterprises of every form of ownership, though they were less frequently employed in firms with wholly Polish capital (see Table 4.12). They found their place in primary labour markets in Poland through three channels – political organisations,

102 *Poland's Post-War Dynamic of Migration*

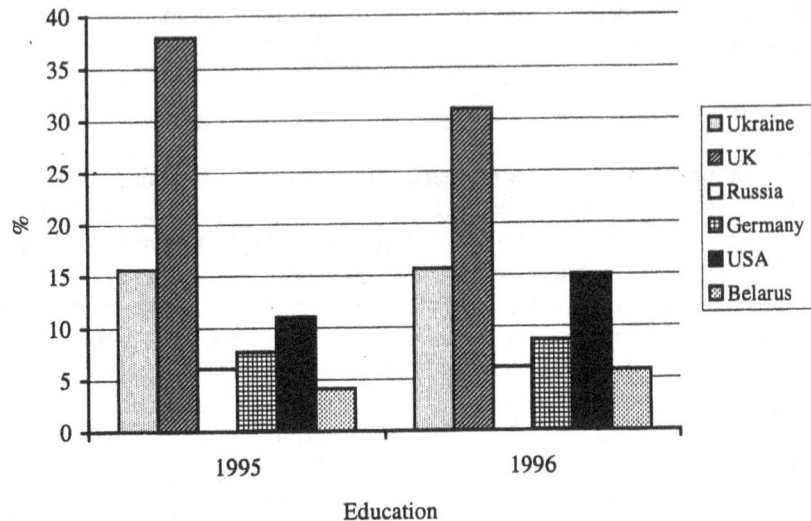

Source: Ministry of Labour Statistics

Figure 4.5e Work permits granted individually by branch of economic activity (main countries of origin) – Education, 1995-1996

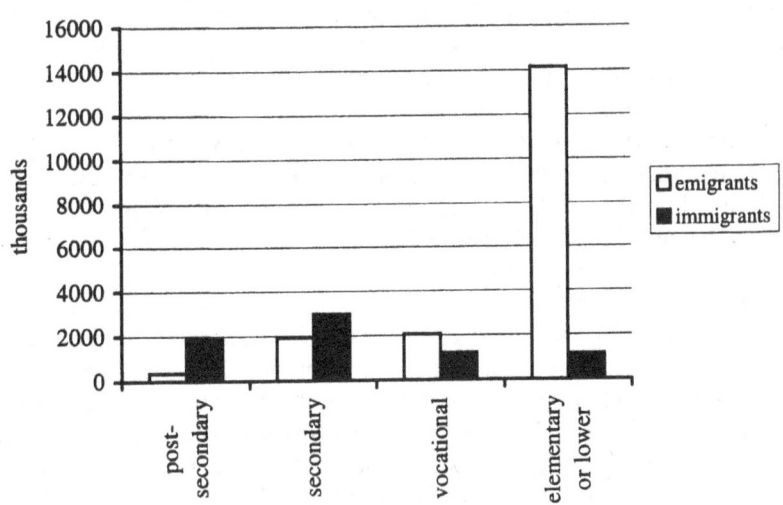

Source: Ministry of Labour Statistics

Figure 4.6 Emigrants and immigrants by educational attainment in Poland, 1996

multinational or joint venture firms and through networks of freelance professionals (Rudolph and Hillman, 1998).

Table 4.13 Work permits for foreigners from Western Europe and the US according to type of work, 1994 and 1995 (%)

Region	Western European Countries and USA		Total	
	1994	1995	1994	1995
All management function	75.0	81.5	1651	2024
Owners	67.0	64.0	633	643
Experts specialist and consultant	49.5	59.9	792	698
Administrative personnel	48.3	55.0	224	68
Medical professions	10.5	57.6	68	115
Teachers trainers	56.8	43.5	532	580
Artists	1.5	2.5	666	542
Skilled manual workers	4.2	26.7	573	65
Unskilled manual workers	0.2	37.5	1816	43
Other	16.6	12.0	177	170

Source: Sprawozdanie z badania sondazowego zezwolenia na prace udzielane cudzoziemcom przez wojewodzkie urzedy pracy w okresie 1994 i 1995, Warsaw, Ministry of Labor Press, 1996

Among international and national organisations hiring foreign experts, one should mention the Poland and Hungary Action for Reconstructing the Economy (PHARE) and the Centrum fur Internationale Migration und Entwicklung (CIM) (the German public recruitment agency for highly skilled manpower).

PHARE focuses on many fields, the most important of which are education and technical assistance for the privatisation process, economic and regional restructuring, human resource development, and infrastructure development. During the first half of the 1990s, Poland received a quarter of the total investment made under the PHARE program (Rudolph and Hillman, 1998), which had been expanded to include other central and eastern European countries. This program had a substantial (but impossible to estimate) number of Western experts stay in Poland (Salt, 1989).

As far as the experts and consultants hired by CIM are concerned, the German government provides funds for topping up their salaries. Since the beginning of the transition, Poland has been the major beneficiary of CIM activities. Experts hired by CIM work mainly in organisations that promote the privatisation process, such as the Polish Development Bank, the Bank for Export Promotion and the Agency for Regional Development (which supports small and medium sized enterprises especially) (Rudolph and Hillman, 1998).

The second channel of West-East migration, namely multinational companies and joint ventures, is of particular significance in shaping the flow of highly skilled professionals in Poland. "Very few of the multinational companies operate without expatriates and sometimes the intention to substitute them is only lip service." (Rudolph and Hillman, 1998, p. 71).

However, very early in the transformation and so at the beginning of many such companies' presence in Poland, there were not enough Poles who could be able to work on the lower executive level (by Western standards) or run certain specific departments like marketing and public relations. Such departments did not exist in the socialist economy and so the domestic highly skilled labour force was not up to the tasks. Therefore, multinationals' strategy was to train Polish personnel in order to replace foreign managers and experts as quickly as possible.[8]

It is also interesting to know who these foreign experts were. Mostly they were expatriates. There were also foreigners who have the same position as the expatriates but who did not benefit from the "expat-package" (such package includes many incentives including free flights home, rental subsidies, etc.). This category is called the "hybrid." "Hybrids" usually have weaker bargaining power at the time of recruitment because, for example, they are already in the country. Common but even less frequent were Polish return migrants, usually children who left with their émigré parents during the Solidarity or martial law period (the first half of 1980s) (Rudolph and Hillman, 1998).

Socio-demographically, this group is predominantly male, relatively young (most often between 30 and 39 years of age), and highly educated. "They come from different background, but all of them are engaged in white-collar professions." (Rudolph and Hillman, 1998, p. 73).

Experts, consultants and teachers dominate the third channel of West-East mobility, i.e. freelance foreigners. The demand for native English speakers at the beginning of transition was very high, not only because the English language is the language of international communication but also because, until 1989, Russian was taught as a first foreign language in Poland. Therefore, there was a huge demand for English language teachers who could quickly be fit into the changes in the educational system. As a result, ten years after the collapse of the system, English is introduced as the first foreign language in kindergartens (though not obligatory at that level), and in the majority of grammar and secondary schools all over the country.

According to Polish Ministry of Labour statistics, the majority of work permits issued to UK nationals were for training and teaching purposes.

"There is an empirical evidence however, that these flows of 'native speakers' are driven not only by the demand in Poland, but also due to the effects of the current recession in Britain" (Rudolph and Hillman, 1998, p. 76).

It is difficult to predict the future of the highly skilled flows from the West into Central Europe. However, the nature and character of this movement and, to some extent, some very recent statistical trends suggest that this kind of mobility will decrease gradually. Some part of the managerial migration will be replaced by short inspection visits, some others by more sophisticated telecommunication. Lastly, Polish managers (already trained by Western colleagues) may travel for instruction or to report activities to the West as well.

Conclusions

The geography of migratory flows into Poland during the transition period reflects the structure of the global division of labour. It is no wonder that, at the beginning of the economic transformation, highly skilled flows from the West and Pacific Rim and only a small part of the flow from the East found employment on the primary labour market. Mobility from the East is characterised mainly by people looking for unskilled or skilled manual work (legal or illegal) on the secondary labour market.

Flows into the primary labour market are highly institutionalised. Immigrants have regulated legal status and are hired to supplement the domestic labour force here, whereas flows from the east reflect rather the dynamic process of migration that transforms temporary entries into settlement. I assume, however, that in the future it will just be immigrants from the East (both from the former Soviet Union and Asia) who will play an important role on both primary and secondary labour markets in Poland. The movement of experts and consultants from the West will diminish gradually but very substantially and will be based more often on an on-off basis than regular stays.

Since the migratory potential lies in the East, the process of migratory globalisation will inevitably increase the flows from the East into Central European countries. In fact, this process has already begun. One should also not forget that economic globalisation will dualise central European labour markets, thereby increasing human mobility and the circulation of capital and goods. What happened in the German, French, Dutch, and other western economies in the 1970s is underway now in the CEE region. It seems that, in the near future, there is going to be a demand or need for foreign labour on central European labour markets. Immigrant communities in Poland have advantageous socio-demographic traits. Migrants' young age, adeptness, skills and occupations mean that the local labour markets should benefit from their presence.

Return Migration from the West

A principle of international migration is that networks between sending and receiving areas are maintained by an ongoing process of return migration comprising both recurrent migrants who regularly go home for varying periods each year and previously settled migrants who settle back in their communities of origin (Massey et al., 1987a). That every migration stream breeds a counter stream (Ravenstain, 1885), and the process of settlement in a receiving area is partially countered by a concomitant return migration (Cornelius, 1978; Mines, 1981) are sociological truisms. However, that which is the norm for migratory behaviour for certain ethnic groups was not visible among the Poles spread all over the world during the communist era.

Before the First and the Second World Wars, many Polish emigrants did return to their homeland (see Table 4.14). Return migration from America to Polish territory prior to the First World War was estimated at approximately 30 per cent of the original emigration (Walaszek, 1984; Pilch and Zgorniak, 1984). The intention of Polish emigrants to return followed one of a few regular patterns: to invest money saved abroad in the old country, to buy land, to build a new house or to set up a small workshop (Walaszek, 1984, p. 213). Some others returned to spend retirement in their home country. After the Second World War, the stream of return migration diminished to a trickle.

Previous sections touched upon the recent return migration of Poles from the West, a phenomenon that was not studied in post-war Poland simply because the numbers of returnees from the West were not significant. Nor are there any statistics concerning the phenomenon of return migration during the communism era. The only data that exists is on overall immigration to Poland. Some part of this movement was undoubtedly return migration. However, it is impossible to give an exact numbers of returnees. Therefore data enclosed in Table 4.15 should not serve as a source of information on return migration of Poles but only as an illustration of trends in overall immigration to Poland during the communist era.

Table 4.14 Permanent departure from the United States to Poland, 1920-1957*

Year	Number	Year	Number
1920	18,190	1939	315
1921	42,207	1940	81
1922	31,004	1941	4
1923	5,278	1942	–
1924	2,590	1943	1
1925	3,693	1944	1
1926	2,823	1945	–
1927	2,725	1946	24
1928	3,046	1947	55
1929	2,316	1948	127
1930	1,924	1949	133
1931	2,101	1950	106
1932	2,375	1951	72
1933	1,627	1952	68
1934	733	1953	71
1935	457	1954	219
1936	443	1955	182
1937	413	1956	67
1938	409	1957	91

* The collection of statistics on emigration from the United States was discontinued in 1957; no direct measure of emigration has been available since then

Source: United States, Department of Justice. Immigration and Naturalization Service, duplicated material. Statistical abstract of the United States, 1939-1957, US Department of Commerce, Washington D.C., Government Printing Office

As mentioned previously, Poles almost always migrated with an intention to come back home someday. The fact that this pattern was broken and a majority of those who emigrated after 1945 did not return may be explained by the state migration policy, i.e. repression towards those (and their family members) who extended their stay abroad.

Since the collapse of the communism in 1989, people wishing to migrate no longer faced the stark choice of "stay or go once, but forever." The disintegration of the communist regime provided a broader range of political freedoms and human rights, such as the right to travel abroad. Polish passport authorities no longer prescribed the duration of a given person's stay abroad. Nor was punishment meted out to those who did not comply by extending their stay abroad. All citizens could keep their passports at home rather than at a police station (Iglicka, 2000a, p. 63).

Table 4.15 Immigration to Poland, 1960-1999 (in thousands)

Year	Numbers	Year	Numbers
1960	5.7	1980	1.5
1961	3.6	1981	1.4
1962	3.3	1982	0.9
1963	2.5	1983	1.2
1964	2.3	1984	1.6
1965	2.2	1985	1.6
1966	2.2	1986	1.9
1967	2.1	1987	1.8
1968	2.2	1988	2.1
1969	2.0	1989	2.2
1970	1.9	1990	2.6
1971	1.7	1991	5.0
1972	1.8	1992	6.5
1973	1.4	1993	5.9
1974	1.4	1994	6.9
1975	1.8	1995	8.1
1976	1.8	1996	8.2
1977	1.6	1997	8.4
1978	1.5	1998	8.9
1979	1.7	1999	9.4

Source: Roczniki Statystyczne (Statistical Yearbooks), Central Statistical Office, GUS, Warsaw, various years

In contemporary Poland, state migration policy does not force potential returnees to rethink their decision about returning more carefully.

During the transition period, the motives that once pulled Polish emigrants to return home still exist; however, a new, qualitative change in this return is observable. The new political, economic and social environments have recently caused new motives and strategies of return to arise. Before this thesis is elaborated upon, let us review theories of return migration. It is important to note at this point that the concept of the return migration cannot, in practice, be defined with great exactness; the distinction between a visit and temporary return, for example, may be very hazy. By "return migrants" I understand all those who declare that they want to spend at least few years in their home country after returning from abroad. It would be splitting hairs to subdivide this category further into those who declare that they will never again migrate abroad and those who say that probably, in a some years, they will migrate again. I believe that the simple event of a "return" (understood here as having restored or rekindled family, job, business or social ties) for an unspecified length of time to a home country should suffice to define a category of return migrants.

"A theory of return migration should be logically derivable as a subset of a more general theory of migration. Unfortunately, the field of migration studies has not generated a generally acceptable theory." (Richmond, 1984, p. 269). Cerase (1974) developed one of the best and commonly accepted typologies of return migration. This typology served in my research as a starting point for an analysis of strategies of return migration of Poles from the USA during the transition period. According to Cerase, there are four types of return migration in theory, although in practice motives may run together:

- *Return of failure* – return migration related to failure to achieve economic goals in the receiving country;
- *Return of conservatism* – return migration governed by a conservative attachment to the values of the sending society. It is this return which comes close to Alberoni and Baglioni's (1965) conception of *emigrazione di rapina*, based on the prospect of going abroad to make a fortune as quickly as possible and then returning home (Cerase, 1974, p. 222);
- *Return of innovation* – return associated with success in the receiving society and 'innovation' on return. It may be said that at some point of their lives abroad, irrespective of the success they achieved in a receiving country, immigrants become conscious of their difference from the local population (it may be because of family or national custom, religion, accent, etc.). They become aware that they cannot go beyond a certain stage, certain social roles are precluded, certain memberships barred, certain types of social advancement impossible. Therefore, some of them may accept the reality of their immigrant status, decide to adapt to it and continue to participate in social life as much as possible, while some others may elect to return to their country of origin. "The return of the emigrants at this point is quite different from the 'return of conservatism' since they achieved a lot in a new society. Both the process of acculturation and that of individual adjustment have reached an advanced stage in this case. With their experience in a new country, they are now prepared and willing to take new values to the old society" (Cerase, 1974, p. 223);
- *Return of retirement* – a return associated with the old age, a feeling of dissatisfaction and/or dis-integration within the receiving society.

Generally speaking, all but one (the third) of the above mentioned types existed before the collapse of communism as rationales of Polish returnees. Those who achieved success and became acculturated to the receiving society (and one has to realise that those tend to be migrants' élite rather than average people) even after becoming aware of "a glass ceiling" tried to adapt to the social barriers rather than return to communist Poland. It is this author's opinion that *return of innovation* is the most important type of return due to emigrants' possible contribution to the home country ("contribution" is not understood here in terms of only finances but likewise of new values, culture, education, skills and/or know-how brought to the old country). This return did not exist before the collapse of the system. However, the political, social and economic transformation caused some successful emigrants to decide to come back to Poland, following the pattern of *return of innovation,* because they started to perceive more economic opportunities for themselves in their home country than in their receiving areas. It may be a case of return in which "migrants return because they have satisfied the goals that they or their family members had set for them or, if they had no specific targets, because they feel that they can now change their original situation in the home country" (Rogers, 1984, p. 289). What is even more interesting, and what makes the case of Polish returnees more complicated, is the fact that this is not, for the most part, a return of the migrants themselves but their children.

Numerous studies have proven that there is little social mobility for the first generation of migrants. Many studies have also shown that the second generation of migrants generally succeeds in a receiving country and is able to move upward on the social ladder much further that their parents were, (Alberoni and Baglioni, 1965; Moynihan 1963; Rogers, 1984) mooting the benefits of a *return of innovation* for emigrants' children. However, a clear case of what can only be termed *return of innovation* by children of Polish migrants has been taking place during the transition period.

In the previously-mentioned 1995 study on managerial mobility from the West to Poland, about one-third of the sample consisted of children of Polish emigrants, most of whom were born in Poland. They have a Polish cultural background, but received their education in the West, often in Anglo-Saxon countries, and were members of *Polonia* (the Polish diaspora who still have family or sentimental ties to Poland).

> A large number of them are coming back now here [Poland]. From the group of people I knew in Canada (there were, with me, four people from my highschool class), around 25 people, already half are back here. Most of them were in professional positions back there. Not the highest. And all of them, except one who opened his own business, are working with multinationals. (General manager of one of the largest multinational software companies), (Rudolph and Hillmann, 1998, p. 73).

In a study on the potential of return migration of Poles from the USA in New York and Philadelphia conducted in 1999 and 2000, this author interviewed leaders of the Polish community's representatives in the USA and conducted 45 in-depth interviews with political and economic migrants and their children who left Poland at the beginning of 1980s.[9] The research hypothesis assumed that the social, economic and political transformation that took place in Poland after 1989 brought about new migratory behaviours and strategies concerning return to the home country. This hypothesis also assumed that types of return migration are correlated with the status and social prestige attained by the migrants in the destination country.

Findings from the interviews with Polish organisations' leaders show that older Polish migrants, those who immigrated to the USA right after the Second World War or in the 1950s and the 1960s, and those who attained a success in the new country do not heed the strategy of a permanent *return of innovation*. Theirs is rather a strategy of establishing business connections in Poland in order to spend some time here and some time there. Those who had emigrated in the 1980s as adults do not also follow permanent *return of innovation* strategies. Nonetheless, patterns indicative of this type of return are followed by the younger generation, who, as little children, immigrated with their parents to the USA.

A very interesting fact observed during the in-depth interviews was a feeling of bitterness and a negative attitude towards changes in Poland observed among the parental generation of Polish emigrants whose children decided to search for the opportunities in the old country.

> He [the speaker's son] got crazy. So, I had to emigrate to leave everything behind, to give him a better life and now he works there. I worked very hard. I took out a loan in order to pay his studying at Stanford and now what? I understand that this is his life and these are his choices but I am not sure whether this all was worth it (Michal, 57, academic at Drexel University).

The feeling of bitterness runs very deep, probably because those who emigrated at the beginning of the 1980s did not expect such rapid changes in Poland. Till the end of the 1980s, they felt that they had made the right choice. At the end of the 1990s, their lives became flustered because some of their children do not approve of their emigration.

> My parents did not speak Polish at home. It is their fault that I cannot speak this language now. They were so strongly against communists that they wanted to forget everything about Poland. I remember that it was always a problem for my grandmother who could not communicate with me when I was a child. Fortunately, now I speak French, she also speaks French so we

can talk. I am thinking about applying for a Polish passport, because definitely in a couple of years I would like to work in Poland or somewhere in Europe. If Poland enters EU, it will mean that I will have a European passport. I do not speak Polish, so this is a problem, but maybe France? I do not want to live here forever (Derek, 28, academic at the University of Pennsylvania, parents: physicians).

It seems that some of the respondents calculated their chances "here" [The U.S.] and "there" [Poland] very cautiously:

I am fluent in English. This is still an advantage and big asset in Poland. But soon all young people will be speaking English, so I want to make the most of this opportunity. I decided to study in Poland, it is better there than here. I started working in Poland (I teach English) so I will pay my tuition by myself. I may achieve a lot there. Here people are so career oriented. Everybody things only about himself. I do not want to participate in this rat race. It's very tiring and frustrating. My parents do not understand that, they stopped talking to me. They do not know that even TV stations are better in Poland (Andrzej, 17, parents: blue collar workers in Philadelphia).

It is definitely not a return related with a feeling of nostalgia or encounter with social barriers in the receiving country. The immigrants' children interviewed were by and large very young, averaging 24 years old. They were also highly educated. The majority held degrees from American universities. It was furthermore not a return related to financial investments in the home country, but the migration was considered as a career move, with further, lasting profit anticipated from it. Some interviewees stressed that their returns are strongly related to the upward carrier mobility easier to achieve in Poland than in the U.S., others stressed that they simply feel much better in Poland.

I did not want to be sent by my firm to any town in the USA they wanted to have a branch. With the exception of New York City, the States is one big hick-ville. I do not like it. So, since I speak Polish, they offered me once a managerial position in Warsaw. I agreed and after two years I decided to stay there and open my own computer firm. My wife is American but she feels good there and my children speak Polish. I travel a lot between Philadelphia and Warsaw but I could never live here forever (Stan, 27 years, parents: dentists).

Of course, the results of this study are not representative and issues of strategies behind return migration require much more quantitative research, both in former receiving areas and in Poland; however, even such a small study shows some new trends and qualitative changes in migratory behaviours on the West-East axis that have occurred during the transition period. This research should also serve as a starting point for further in depth analysis on areas such as social and institutional problems encountered by returnees, since in every kind of migration, even return migration, there are always problems in adapting and adjustment.

> There was just a small group of us who felt that people returning from abroad had certain things in common in terms of their outlook, but also in terms of having to adjust to Poland after return – despite the fact that most people travelled to Poland quite often and obviously had friends and relatives here. Nevertheless, when you actually return to stay here permanently, you then do at first feel a little bit alienated in that you have got used to something else abroad than what you actually find here in Poland. Communist propaganda for so many years was that anyone who leaves Poland was a bit of a traitor. It has taken its toll. That perception is still there... (Manager of one of the Polish return migrants' clubs in Warsaw), (Rudolph and Hillman, 1998, p. 73).

Another dimension of migration on the West-East axis is the return migration from Germany to southern-western territories of Poland (Silesia) by people with dual citizenship. These are people who emigrated to Germany in the 1970s and the 1980s as so called *Spataussiedlers* (late emigrants).[10] Relative to other Polish emigrant groups in Germany, this group comprised chiefly young, dynamic and highly educated people. It included engineers, doctors, scientists, managers and teachers, as well as artists, musicians, etc. (Heffner, 1999). They (as a whole) did not give up their Polish citizenship despite living for years in Germany and having been granted German citizenship.

Some of these emigrants are deciding to return to Poland now. The number of such returns numbers 1,500-2,000 annually (Heffner, 1999). But it is still a tentative return. Their German passport now gives them an opportunity to work in Germany (seasonally, for a half of a year or so) and benefit from the German social welfare system while investing their earnings in Poland. They set up businesses here, suggesting that in the nearest future they will probably spend most of the year in Poland. "They are trying to make the most of the professional skills and contacts gained in the German economic system" (Heffner, 1999, p. 193). The representative of German Minority Society in Opole Silesia, senator Gerhard Bartodziej said:

> This is the beginning of the process only. But returns to Upper Silesia will happen in the tens of thousands soon. Those people who left the region during the last few years, those who did not get rid of all they had, those who have dual citizenship and homes here will come back to Upper Silesia soon (Heffner, 1999, p. 204).

So far, returnees have been moving into the larger urban centres, mostly to Opole. Return migration to rural areas occurs on a relatively low level. The disappearing differences between living and working conditions between Poland and Germany, a process that has already begun, may favour a future, permanent *return of innovation* in larger numbers of those who did not re-root themselves in Germany. The estimated number of such potential returnees is around 200,000 (Heffner, 1999). So far however, short and long-term migrations to Germany in order to work have become a significant and stimulating factor in the development of the regional economy.

Notes

1   As a result of the understanding reached by European Union member countries in September 1995, all of the countries of the former Soviet Union (as opposed to the other non-Soviet former Communist bloc countries) were put on the "visa-rule list."
2   The least frequent channel belonged to applications for asylum.
3   Recently, the first case was brought to the court where lawyer's office was accused of helping to arrange for fictitious marriages of foreigners with Polish citizens (Tor, 1999).
4   The new Constitution (1997) contains an article (art. 35) on the protection of national and ethnic minorities that states:
    1. The Republic of Poland ensures Polish citizens belonging to national and ethnic minorities the freedom to maintain and develop their own language, to maintain their own customs and traditions, and to develop their own culture.
    2. National and ethnic minorities have the right to establish educational and cultural institutions, institutions designed to protect religious identity, as well as to participate in the resolution of matters connected with their cultural identity.
    The said article contains a proactive commitment of the state to ensure minority members have the right to maintain and develop their own culture (language, traditions, customs) and grants them the right to establish organisations and participate in making decisions aimed at maintaining their own culture and religion. The Constitution restricts the protection of minority rights to people possessing Polish citizenship, at the same time providing separate protection of the rights of foreigners (article 56). Such a "citizen's clause" conforms to the standards of minority protection established within the European framework (OSCE, the Council of Europe). The provisions of that article also uphold an individualised approach to the protection of minorities by using a phrase "Polish citizens belonging to national or ethnic minorities which is consistent with currently existing international standards. Legal regulations adopted in the provisions of the new Constitution regarding the protection of rights of national minorities are also in conformity with provisions regarding minorities issues contained in constitutions of other states in Central Europe (Janicki, 1995; Kranz, 1998).
5   This section was published in Iglicka, 2000c.
6   The new Act was passed in 1998.
7   The project was conducted in co-operation with the Center for Migration Research, Warsaw University. During this study, semi-structured interviews were conducted with

high-level managers in some 50 multinational companies/joint ventures, as well as interviews with experts, managers and professionals (for details see Rudolph and Hillman, 1998).
8   In the here-mentioned study, the average stay of foreign managers and experts was about two or three years.
9   This study was conducted during my stay as a Senior Fulbright Fellow at the Population Studies Center of the University of Pennsylvania.
10 The term *Spataussiedler* refers to a person who emigrated in the 1970s or the 1980s. German terminology distinguishes between earlier and later émigrés since the cultural, social and motivational factors in their emigration to Germany were clearly different from those which characterized the earlier *'Aussiedler'* group. It is stressed in the literature now that the economic factor played a very important role in this group's emigration from Poland (Heffner, 1999).

References

Alberoni, F. and Baglioni, G. (1965), *L'integrazione dell'immigrato nella societa industriale*, Il Mulino, Bolognia.
Babinski, G. (2000), 'The Ukrainians in Poland after the Second World War', in F.E.I. Hamilton and K. Iglicka (eds), *From Homogeneity to Multiculuralism. Minorities Old and New in Poland*, SSEES, University of London, London.
Castles, S. (1995), 'How nation-states respond to immigration and ethnic diversity', *New Community*, vol. 3, no. 21, pp. 293-308.
Castles, S. and Miller, M.J. (1993), *The Age of Migration: International Population Movements in the Modern World*, Macmillan, London.
Cerase, F. (1977), 'Nostalgia or Disenchantment: Considerations on Return Migration', in S.M. Tomasi and M.H. Engel (eds), *The Italian experience in the United States*, Center for Migration Studies, New York.
Chesnais, J.C. (1993), 'Soviet emigration: Past, Present and Future', in *The changing course of international migration*, OECD, Paris.
Condominas, G. and Pottier, R. (1983), *Les refugies originares de l'Asia du Sud-Est*, Rapport au President de la Republique, la Documentation Francaise.
Cornelius, W.A. (1978), 'Mexican Migration to the United States, Consequences and US Responses', *Migration and Development Monograph*.
Department for Migration and Refugee Affairs' statistics (1999), Ministry of Interior and Administration, Warsaw.
Department of Justice. Immigration and Naturalization Service, United States 1939-1957 (1957), US Department of Commerce, Washington D.C., Government Printing Office.
Edwards, R.C. (1975), 'The Social Relations of Production in the Firm and Labor Market Structure', in R.C. Edwards, M. Reich and D.M. Gordon (eds), *Labor Market Segmentation*, D.C. Heath, Lexington.
Frejka, T. (1996), *International Migration in Central and Eastern Europe and the Commonwealth of Independent States*, United Nations, New York and Geneva.
Glytsos, N. (2000), 'Aspects of Economic Integration of Ethnic Greek Immigrants', paper presented at the IZA Workshop on Ethnic Migrants in Labour Market and Society, Bonn, Germany, 29-31 January.
Gordon, D.M. (1972), *Theories of Poverty and Underemployment: Orthodox, Radical and Dual Labor Market Perspectives*, D.C. Heath, Lexington.

Halik, T. (1995), *Wyniki badan ankietowych prowadzonych w srodowisku imigrantow wietnamskich* (The results of the survey conducted among Vietnamese immigrants), typescript, ISS UW, Warsaw.
Halik, T. (2000), 'The Vietnamese in Poland. Images/Scenes from the Past, Present and Future', in F.E.I. Hamilton and K. Iglicka, *From Homogeneity to Multiculuralism. Minorities Old and New in Poland*, SSEES, University of London, London.
Hamilton, F.E.I. and Iglicka, K. (eds) (2000), *From Homogeneity to Multiculturalism. Minorities Old and New in Poland*, SSEES, University of London, London.
Heffner, K. (1999), 'The Return of Emigrants from Germany to Upper Silesia: Reality and Prospects', in K. Iglicka and K. Sword (eds), *The Challenge of East-West Migration for Poland*, Macmillan, London.
Iglicka, K. (1998c), 'Are They Fellow Country-Men or Not? The Migration of Ethnic Poles from Kazakhstan to Poland', *International Migration Review*, vol. 32, no. 4 (Winter), pp. 995-1015.
Iglicka, K. (2000a), 'Mechanisms of migration from Poland before and during the transition period', *Journal of Ethnic and Migration Studies*, vol. 26, no. 1, pp. 61-73.
Iglicka, K. (2000c), 'Ethnic Division on Emerging Foreign Markets in Poland', *Europe-Asia Studies*, vol. 52, no. 7, pp. 1237-55.
Iglicka, K. (forthcoming a), 'Migration From and Into Poland in the Light of East-West European Migration', *International Migration*.
Iglicka, K. (forthcoming b), 'The Revival of Ethnic Consciousness: a Case of Poland', *Migracje i Spoleczenstwo*, vol. 4, IH PAN, Warsaw.
Iglicka, K., Jazwinska, E., Kepinska, E. and Korys, P. (1997), 'Imigranci w Polsce w swietle badania etnosondazowego' (Immigrants in Poland in the light of ethnosurvey), *Working Paper*, no. 10, ISS UW, Warsaw.
Janicki, L. (1995), 'Status mniejszosci narodowych w konstytucjach krajow srodkowo- i wschodnioeuropejskich' (The status of national minorities in constitutions of Central and East European countries), *Przeglad Zachodni*, no. 4, pp. 24-31.
Jedlicki, J. (1999), 'Historical memory as a source of conflicts in Eastern Europe', *Communist and Post Communist Studies*, vol. 32, no. 3, pp. 228-29.
Jerczynski, M. (1999), 'Patterns of Spatial Mobility of Citizens of the Former Soviet Union', in K. Iglicka and K. Sword (eds), *The Challenge of East-West Migration for Poland*, Macmillan, London.
Kotkin, J. (1993), *The Human Races: How Race, Religion and Self-Identity Influence Success in the New Global Economy*, Random House, New York.
Kozlowski, T.K. (1999), 'Migration Flows in the 1990s: Challenges for Entry, Asylum and integration Policy in Poland', in K. Iglicka and K. Sword (eds), *The Challenge of East-West Migration for Poland*, Macmillan, London.
Kranz, J. (ed) (1998), *Law and Practice of Central European Countries in the Field of National Minorities Protection after 1989*, Center for International Relations, Warsaw.
Kwilecki, A. (1963), 'Mniejszosci narodowe w Polsce Ludowej' (National Minorities in Peoples' Republic), *Kultura i Spoleczenstwo*, no. 4, pp. 87-8.
Marciniak, T. (2000), 'Armenians in Poland after 1989', in F.E.I. Hamilton and K. Iglicka (eds), *From Homogeneity to Multiculuralism. Minorities Old and New in Poland*, SSEES, University of London, London.
Massey, D.S., et al. (1987a), *Return to Aztlan: The social process of International Migration from Western Mexico*, University of California, Berkley.
Massey, D.S., et al. (1993), 'Theories of International Migration: Review and Appraisal', *Population and Development Review*, vol. 19, no. 3, pp. 431-65.
Michalska, A. (1997), 'Pracownicy-migranci jako "nowa" mniejszosc narodowa' (Immigrants-workers as a "new" minority), *Sprawy Narodowosciowe. Seria Nowa*, no. 1, pp. 96-104.

Migration in Central and Eastern Europe – Review (1999), IOM, Geneva.
Mines, R. (1981), 'Developing a Community Tradition of Migration: a Field Study in Rural Zacatecas, Mexico and California Settlement Areas', *US-Mexican Studies*, no. 3, pp. 15-19.
Moynihan, D.P. (1963), *Beyond the Melting Pot*, The M.I.T. Press, Cambridge.
Okolski, M. (1995), *Trends in International Migrations. Poland: the 1995 SOPEMI Report*, OECD, Paris.
Okolski, M. (1996), *Trends in International Migrations. Poland: the 1996 SOPEMI Report*, OECD, Paris.
Okolski, M. (1997), 'New migration trends in Central and Eastern Europe in the 1990s', *ISS Working Papers*, no. 4, Warsaw.
Okolski, M. (1998a), 'Regional dimension of international migration in Central and Eastern Europe', *Genus*, vol. LIV, no. 1-2, pp. 11-37.
Okolski, M. (1998c), *Recent trends in international migration – Poland 1998*, SOPEMI report, Paris.
Pilch, A. and Zgorniak, M. (eds) (1984), *Emigracja z ziem polskich w czasach nowozytnych i najnowszych* (Emigration from Polish lands in modern and contemporary times), PWN, Warsaw.
Piore, M.J. (1979), *Birds of Passage: Migrant Labor and Industrial Societies*, Cambridge Univeristy Press, Cambridge.
Poland – statistical data on migration 1994-1998 (1999), Office for Migration and Refugees, Warsaw.
Portes, A. (1981), 'Modes of Structural Incorporation and Present Theories of Labour Immigration', in M.M. Kritz, C.B. Keely and S.M. Tomasi (eds), *Global Trends in Migration*, Center for Migration Studies, New York.
Ravenstein, E.G. (1885), 'The Laws of Migration', *Journal of the Royal Statistical Society*, no. 52.
Richmond, A.H. (1984), 'Explaining Return Migration', in D. Kubat (ed), *The Politics of Return. International Return Migration in Europe*, New York: Center for Migration Studies.
Roczniki Statystyczne (Statistical yearbooks), (various years), GUS (Central Statistical Office), Warsaw.
Rogers, R. (1984), 'Return migration in a comparative perspective', in D. Kubat (ed), *The Politics of Return. International Return Migration in Europe*, Center for Migration Studies, New York.
Rudolph, H. and Hillman, F. (1998), 'The Invisible Hand Needs Visible Heads: Managers, Experts and Professionals from Western Countries in Poland', in K. Koser and H. Lutz (eds), *Social Constructions and Social Realities*, Macmillan, London.
Sprawozdanie z badania sondazowego zezwolenia na prace udzielane cudzoziemcom przez wojewodzkie urzedy pracy w okresie 1994-1995 (30 czerwiec), 1995 (1996), Ministry of Labor Press, Warsaw.
Tor, K. (1999), 'Polsko-Wietnamska fikcja malzenska' (Polish-Vietnamese marital fiction), 'Rzeczypospolita', 19 October.
Walaszek, A. (1984), 'Return Migration from the USA to Poland', in D. Kubat (ed), *The Politics of Return. International Return Migration in Europe*, Center for Migration Studies, New York.

5 Summary

European East-West migration, a phenomenon neglected in the past by researchers and policy makers, has recently become a controversial and extremely important topic for the international community. The growing number of international meetings and conferences devoted to indicates the issue's significance. In particular, the spectre of uncontrolled mass emigration from Eastern Europe sparked public debate in the West.

I strongly agree with Castles and Miller's (1993, p. 12) statement that

> ...migration played an extremely important part in the political transformation of Central and Eastern Europe. The collapse of East Germany had a 'domino effect' upon other communist regimes. The political transformation of the region enabled hundreds of thousands to emigrate. During 1989 alone, some 1.2 million people left the former Warsaw Pact area.

causing a perceived threat among well-established Western European societies. One should, however, remember that a Central and Eastern European migration system did exist prior to the collapse of communist rule and migratory movements in this part of Europe had their own dynamics. Unfortunately, most experts treat 1989 as a starting point for studies of changes in population mobility dynamics in the region. This often leads to ad-hoc and primarily short-perspective analyses of East-West migration. Such an approach does not permit full understanding of the complexity of new population movements in the region, nor does it help to understand their dynamics. It is common knowledge that social and demographic processes do not occur in a vacuum but are rooted in the past, but so far this seems to have been overlooked in studying Eastern Europe. This book is the first attempt to examine population mobility in the CEE region generally, and in Poland particularly, from a relatively long perspective encompassing the whole post-Second World War period.

A widely adopted typology of the migration systems in Europe lists three systems on the continent only. They are as follows:

- the Western European migration system that comprises Switzerland, the small states of Andorra, Liechtenstein, Monaco and San Marino,

and all countries of the current European Union with the exception of the United Kingdom and Ireland,
- the United Kingdom and Ireland migration system with its stronger migration ties with countries of the British Commonwealth and Pakistan than with other countries of continental Europe and,
- the Nordic migration system, including such countries as Denmark, Finland, Iceland, Norway and Sweden (Kritz and Zlotnik, 1992, pp. 37-8).

Any attempt to analyse the trends and mechanisms of migration taking place in a wider European setting and referring to a systems approach had, by necessity, to omit the CEE region. Thus the notion of an Eastern and/or Central and Eastern migration system has hardly been construed in the literature. An attempt to fill this gap was undertaken in this book as well. Moreover, one of the aims of this volume was to analyse the scale, forms, causes and mechanisms of migration in what was called the "Second-World," so often neglected in the topical literature.

The time span used here in the analysis of mechanisms and patterns of migration in the CEE region stretches back to 1945. Poles' emigratory trends, types and strategies were examined according to established subperiods for the whole post-war period. Cultural, historical and social ties linking Poland with its traditional destination countries and countries that recently started sending migrants to Poland were carefully examined here. This provided opportunities to make a comprehensive analysis of the political, economic and social mechanisms that are gradually turning one of the biggest and most important sending areas in Central and Eastern Europe into a country of net-immigration and transit. The broader perspective also facilitated a better understanding of the nature of international migration flows stemming from the penetration of capitalist economic relations into peripheral countries where non-market or pre-market social and economic structures once prevailed.

After the collapse of the communism, in barely a decade, old mechanisms of population mobility in Poland have been disturbed and replaced or significantly supplemented by entirely new mechanisms. Variables listed in the migration system approach such as social context (differences in the standard of living or welfare and migrant networks), wage and price differences or short-term travel links (see Figure 1.1, p. 3) and, on the other hand, Western European countries' stricter migration policy towards flux from the former Soviet Union have been playing a crucial role in the dramatic increase in intra-system population mobility. Since 1989, the "Central European" part of the system has been connected with the Western European migration system through bilateral fluxes of people. Fluxes from the West have been likewise quite visible in the eastern part of this system; however, streams in the opposite direction (from Eastern to Western Europe) have been restrained and limited by policy regulations. This causes some ripples on the Central and Eastern European migration system's surface and might lead, in my opinion, to its future possible break-up. If the system does not disintegrate, Poland will probably belong to two systems simultaneously, which will make an analysis of future migration trends in this country even more intriguing.

* * *

In this concluding part, I first examine major findings that stem from the analysis of social and demographic characteristics of permanent and temporary migration from Poland during the post-war period. Special emphasis is put here on patterns and mechanisms of the outflows in the period before and during the transition. Then, by means of a description of the in-depth mechanisms that are converting temporary stays by various categories of foreigners in Poland into permanent ones, I summarise major findings stemming from the immigration pattern analysis. Common consequences of foreigners' presence in a given country, such as the formation of immigrant communities and social inequalities on labour markets, are considered here as well. Stress is put on fluxes and ethnicity of foreigners now in Poland who, after the European Union (EU) enlargement, may possibly be excluded from the expanded Western European migration system.

As already mentioned, for more than a century Poland has been one of the biggest sending areas in Central and Eastern Europe and a vast reservoir of labour for many countries in Western Europe and North America. Irrespective of whether the motive of emigration was political or economic, Poles almost always migrated with the intention to return home. The fact that the majority of them did not actually do so may be explained chiefly by Poland's former political and socio-economic environment. This is especially true in case of the years 1945-1989 when Polish passport authorities prescribed the duration of a given person's stay abroad; many people wishing to migrate faced the stark choice of "stay or go, but forever." During the whole communist era, Germany was the major European destination country for Polish emigration (in fact, emigration to that country reached exodus proportions in the late 1980s). The major overseas destination, and second most popular end-destination overall, was the USA. However, since emigration to the USA averaged only slightly more than 10 per cent of all emigrants in the post-war period, one may say that if it were not for emigration to Germany, emigration from Poland would not represent a statistically significant issue.

Due to the massive westward outflow (and to Germany in particular), Poland undoubtedly gravitated towards the Western European migration system. The uni-directional nature of this movement however, precluded its membership therein. Poland's geographic and political situation pre-destined it to struggle literally between the West and the East. As to relations with the West that shaped ex-Poland population mobility, German colonisation and hegemony over some part of ethnically or historically Polish territory spanning many decades obviously had a bearing on ties and relations between the ethnic populations in the region. A further aspect is the massive emigration to Germany relates to events of the Second World War. At that time, the German authorities introduced a list of ethnic Germans (Volksliste) into which the people of Upper Silesia and Gdansk Pomerania (the Corridor) were forcibly entered, and parts of the populations of other conquered territories were recruited with promises of better life. Several hundred thousand Germans from eastern and southern Europe were also resettled onto Polish territory as part of operation "Heim ins Reich" (Home in the Reich). These categories of citizens, i.e. Volksdeutsche and their descendants, German resettlers from further east, but primarily a considerable part of the native Slavic population of Upper Silesia, Warmia and Masuria – constitute what is called the German minority in contemporary Poland (Kurcz, 2000).

During the expulsion period of 1946-1950, more than two million of them were expelled (Ociepka, 1994; Kurcz, 1997). The years 1956-1957 are known as the "October thaw" because in October 1956 there were several attempts by the new, Post-Stalinist communist authorities to democratise communism; for the German minority this meant a right to emigrate. It caused a wave of departures for Germany: approximately 217,000 people who claimed to be German emigrated – a number equivalent to almost all the Germans then living in Poland.

The social reality proved to be more complicated yet since, with the passage of time, thousands of applications for permission to leave for the Federal Republic of Germany were made, motivated by families' desire to reunite or by a suddenly "discovered" German ancestry. This process accelerated rapidly when the Poland-FRG treaty of 1970 permitted 179,000 people to leave for West Germany. One should also remember the fact that, in the 1980s, emigration (mainly illegal) to Germany (of ethnic Germans, their family members and those who simply took advantage of the lenient policy of the Federal Republic of Germany towards the application for *Aussiedler* status) represented an opportunity to live better, and people just simply made the most of it. Official Polish statistics indicate that around

271,000 people emigrated legally between 1980 and 1989; the estimated actual number (Okolski, 1994) for this period was 1.1-1.3 million (the majority of them to Germany). The outflow to Germany accelerated especially in 1988 and in 1989 when forthcoming restrictions in German migration policy were expected (Iglicka, 2000a). Although German registers show that the number of Poles who applied for *Aussiedler* status, which had *de facto* amounted to a major component of total Polish citizens immigrating to Germany for 40 years, dropped dramatically in the 1990s, stricter regulations introduced by the German government towards emigration based on ethnic claims did not diminish the registered outflow from Poland to Germany in the 1990s.

The future of emigration to Germany depends mainly on the economic situation of Poland. Phenomena recently observed in Poland, such as a return migration from Germany and waning interest in belonging to German minority organisations suggest that emigration to Germany based on ethnic claims may further significantly decrease in the nearest future. However, emigration based on family reunification will still be visible in statistics, though its size will be economically dependent.

Who emigrated from post-war Poland? Emigration from Poland, whether internationally-agreed or forcibly imposed, by Germans, Ukrainians and Jews right after the Second World War was made up mostly of women, children and the elderly. Episodes of emigration to Israel in the 1950s and 1960s were typically of whole families and so sex and age structures of emigrants were quite evenly distributed. Registered outflow to Germany was based either on application for *Aussiedler* status or on family reunification claims; here women and the youngest cohorts were slightly more numerous. Generally, however, during the years 1945-1989 women dominated significantly over men in the official registers. This was due to the pattern, characteristic of the communist era, of illegal (unregistered) male departure (under the guise of tourists) followed by legal female emigration.

In the 1980s, emigration became the domain of young and very young cohorts, for the most part urban and well educated. Brain drain was a major problem; as many as 15 per cent of Polish academics, most frequently computer scientists, physicists and biologists, either permanently emigrated or left the country on long-term contracts.

This changed during the transformation period, which brought a lot of opportunities for dynamic, well educated, and young urban cohorts, the same segments of society that had been the most prone to migrate. Therefore, settlement-oriented emigration from Poland declined in the 1990s. Official registers confirm this, showing that, during the transition period, emigration was at its lowest level since 1960 (with the small exception of

1970-1974). Emigration in the 1990s was about 40 per cent lower than the 1985-1989 average and almost 20 per cent under the 1980-1984 average. However, the political, social and economic transformation brought about economic hardship for some segments of society, especially the working class, rural dwellers, the middle aged and the poorly educated. So the opportunities and difficulties the economic transformation brought affected migration structures after the collapse of the communism.

After almost 50 years of females' excess over males in official statistics, the number of males became significantly higher than the number of females in the first half of the 1990s. This tendency was maintained in the second half of the decade, meaning that the 1980s pattern of illegal male migration followed by legal female migration had been abandoned. It also suggests that unregistered emigration from Poland – a stream that is absolutely impossible to be measured or estimated – must have declined in the 1990s as well. Another peculiar characteristic of emigration in the transition period is a higher frequency, and now in fact the predominance, of people in the middle of productive age.

The general level of education of the Polish populace has been constantly on the rise throughout the 1990s. Despite this, the lowly educated were not only the largest category of emigrants, but their numbers constantly were on the rise. This represents one of the most important changes to the emigrants' demographic structure.

On the basis of the official statistical data, the geography of migration seems to be the sole significant similarity in emigration from Poland before and during the transition period. Germany and the USA are still the major receiving areas of Polish migrants. As far as sending areas are concerned, Polish migrants still come from the most populous, most industrialised, and urbanised regions.

Other sources only in part confirm trends observed in the official statistics. Although those sources do not allow an estimate of outflow volume, they constitute ample grounds to explain its mechanisms and reveal new trends invisible in official records. The most important finding from an ethnosurvey on Poles' mobility is that the main types of mobility in the pre-transition period, i.e. shuttle and permanent migration, have remained in the fore during the transition period. The rapid decline of long-term migration (lasting over one year), and a sudden rise of short-term migration (from 3 months to 1 year) however, would appear to indicate a changing trend in income-generating migrations. The transition from long-term migration, predominantly to Germany or overseas destinations such as the USA and Canada, to short-term migration to (aside from Germany, which is still the most common choice) Austria, Belgium, Italy or Greece is noticeable. One of the favourable conditions for this was the market-based revaluation of the zloty that caused migration's profitability to plummet.

The outflow from Poland in the 1990s coincided with the liberalisation of Polish state migration policy. However, it also coincided with stricter regulations on migrant workers and immigration based on ethnic claims in northwestern Europe. These external, regulatory hurdles did not significantly reduce the registered outflow from Poland, but they did reduce the unregistered outflow and radically changed Poles' strategies behind short- or long-term, income-generating migration. The other factor that changed mechanisms of this kind of migration was the economic hardship inflicted by the political, economic and social transformations on some segments of Polish society. Austerities and hardship inclined those people to view international migration as one of very few ways to preserve their existing level of consumption. Motives that were once commonly behind Poles' income-generating migration, such as to accumulate capital in order to set up commercial activities back home or to enhance their standard of living after returning home, became less apparent in the transition period. In fact, a striving to maintain the level of consumption through international income-generating migration is now contributing to a weakening of family ties (many such migrants are women), and an increase in autarchic circles of family and neighbours. The same striving is also, on the macro-level, undermining of the public sphere and contributing to both economic and social stagnation in some regions of Poland.

Another very interesting finding is that, contrary to that of the permanent outflow, the geography of short- and long-term income-generating migration changed dramatically during the transition period. This pertains to both sending and receiving areas. People who are involved in this kind of migration are mainly inhabitants of backward rural areas and small towns from northeastern or southeastern regions of Poland. In the past, they were less prone to migrate because of the minimum level of social security provided by the state and the lack of the unemployment.

Legal obstacles encountered by Polish migrant workers in the majority of northwestern European countries as well as economic recession and its resulting surplus of local and foreign labour in these countries caused traditional destination areas for Polish income-seeking migrants to become less accessible. However, favourable conditions for cheap, illegal foreign workers were found on the secondary labour markets in Austria, Belgium and especially Italy and Greece. There were many factors conducive to the rapid increase of Poles' income-generating migration to these two Mediterranean countries. Their economies' high seasonality (especially in construction, tourism and agriculture), and the continuing exodus of Italians and Greeks from low-status jobs played important roles in this process. Secondly, as already stated, social processes do not and did not appear in a vacuum. The first larger flux of Poles to Italy and Greece took place in 1981 after the introduction of the martial law in Poland. From then into the mid-eighties thousands of refugees found shelter and a sense of welcome and therefore security. Polish clubs and institutions, and thus a migrant network, started to flourish and, by the end of 1980s, had created favourable conditions for subsequent waves of migration. As Massey (1999, p. 306) describes:

> When an immigration stream begins, it displays a strong tendency to continue because of the growth and elaboration of migrant networks. The concentration of immigrants in certain destination areas creates a "family and friends" effect that channels later streams of immigrants to the same places and facilitates their arrival and integration. If enough migrants arrive under favourable conditions, an enclave economy may form, which further augments the specialised demand for immigrant workers.

This is exactly what happened in the case of Polish income-generating migration to Italy and Greece.

As far as immigration is concerned, economic literature acknowledges that it is one of the most advantageous factors of and a force in restructuring processes of economies worldwide. By the end of 1980s, most highly developed countries had become diverse, multiethnic societies, and those that have not reached this stage yet are moving decisively in that direction (Massey et al., 1993).

Since 1989, along with the social, political and economic transformation and the collapse of the Soviet empire, factors conducive not only to the decline in the human outflow but also to the increase in the inflow into Poland have occurred. Economic globalisation has brought about a dualisation of central European labour markets, thereby contributing to the increase in the circulation of people, capital and goods. Thus Poland, a central European latecomer to the global stage, has slowly begun to convert from being a major sending country into a country of net-immigration and transit. The conversion is following the patterns that have already been established in other European countries.

Similarly to the example set by Southern European countries that changed from mass emigration areas into mass immigration regions in the 1980s (King and Rybaczuk, 1993), important factors in Poland have been as follows:

- the ease of entry into Poland by people from the former Soviet Union;
- the geographical, cultural and linguistic proximity between Poland and many of the newly independent countries of the former Soviet Union;

- divergent standards of living and differences in exchange rates and price relations;
- (economic restructuring and a dualisation of labour markets with a consequent large grey market for cheap, flexible immigrant labour on the one hand and a need for highly skilled professionals on the other.

The movement into Poland is predominantly from the East; some recent trends in population mobility may be explained by past trends and migratory dynamics. Indeed, a statement by Kritz and Zlotnik (1992, p. 4) that '...in studying international migration systems, one has to consider not only the spatial dimension that demarcated all countries in a system, but a time dimension is also essential to capture flow and counter-flow dynamics. Thus, a historical perspective is required...' is very true in the case of Poland. Let us therefore consider recent population movements from the migration systems perspective.

As it was already explained, political circumstances after 1945 forced Poland into the Eastern European migration system. Within this system, flows among former communist block countries, albeit relatively moderate, were mutual and quite diverse, although entirely regulated by state apparatuses. This encompassed tourism, student exchanges, the mobility of migrant workers within the COMECON framework, repatriation processes of selected minorities, military movements, etc.

Irrespective of the new political system imposed on Poland in 1945 by the Soviet Union, strong historical and cultural ties between Poland and the "East" indisputably bound (for good and bad) populations in this region. It is enough to mention that in the last pre-war census (1931), there were around 6.5 million people of "eastern" descent, such as Belarussians, Ukrainians, Lithuanians, Russians, Armenians, Tartars or Karaites of Poland's then-total population of 32 million (Rocznik Statystyczny, 1932). Therefore, Poland's belonging to the Eastern European migration system was not something absolutely unfitting or unfounded.

In contemporary Poland, the Ukrainian ethnic group has been estimated at around 250,000 strong, making it the second (after the German) largest ethnic group. Other "eastern" ethnic groups in Poland are Belarussians (230,000), Lemkos (60,000), Lithuanians (20,000), Russians (15,000), Armenians (3,000), Tartars (4,000) and Karaites (fewer than 1000) (Kwilecki, 1988). The presence of the Ukrainian group was, in my opinion, a catalyst the recent wave of settlement or long-term migration from Ukraine to Poland. Another conducive factor to this immigration is the rather peaceful coexistence of Poles and Ukrainians in post-communist Poland. Therefore, despite an acrimonious history, there are no big hurdles based on the ethnic prejudice towards the "new" immigration from Ukraine into Poland that has been underway since 1989.

Migratory pressure exerted by newly-mobile Eastern Europeans, its further demographic potentiality and Western Europe's restrictive migration policies were all conducive to the formation of a migration buffer zone in post-communist Central Europe in the 1990s. The zone may represent the beginning of the end for the old, joint Central and Eastern European migration system.

The most important inflow into post-communist Poland was the brief, mass international movement of citizens of the former Soviet Union. This movement can be termed *primitive mobility*. This new social phenomenon of people being systematically "on the move" stemmed largely from differentials in exchange rates and prices between Poland and post-Soviet countries, compounded and magnified by a shortage of basic goods in the latter. However, the new and widespread spatial mobility of citizens of the former Soviet Union was not a social and demographic blip but a harbinger of real immigration. At first, the *primitive mobility* was perceived mainly as a threat by Central Europeans, whose countries had become destinations for masses of Eastern Europeans. Eventually, that mobility revealed more positive than negative aspects. The enormous circulation of visitors from the former Soviet Union who came to Poland to buy products for export and re-export brought such benefits as an inflow of foreign currency, partial mitigation of a chronically negative official balance of payments, local economic development in a number of regions, an increase in job opportunities in those regions, enhanced competition on labour markets, etc. Recently, after a decade of penetration of Polish merchandise and labour markets by petty-traders and seasonal workers from the East, one can observe that many of those people, having come to terms with restrictions in Western Europe against mobility from the "East," have started contemplating long-term or permanent residence in Poland. This is especially true for especially workers and traders who have already established networks in Poland. Migrant networks undoubtedly play a very important role in this. However, one should also realise that, so far, Polish migration policy has been an important determinant behind the increased mobility and immigration from the East. For example, citizens of the former Soviet Union do not need visas to enter Poland. A January 1998 attempt to introduce stricter regulations towards movement from the East (mainly to gradually adapt domestic immigration policy to E.U. standards in the pre-accession period) had to be modified quickly when it turned out that, for the time being, there are more positive than negative aspects of *primitive mobility* from the former Soviet Union in Poland.

Nevertheless, the slow conversion of some part of the mass international mobility into immigration has been triggered. During the 1990s, there was an intensive penetration of Polish trade and labour markets by people from the former Soviet Union with this came the founding of strong networks channelling the inflows from the East. And so the dynamic process of migration has already re-oriented the formerly temporary entry of many seasonal workers, petty-traders or asylum seekers into entry with settlement intentions.

There are a variety of ways whereby this phenomenon has been legitimised. The most obvious are by legal procedures leading to permanent residence, permission to work or becoming acknowledged as a lawful resident of Poland by marrying a Polish citizen or by becoming a repatriated person. Since the collapse of the communism, growing trends in all these channels have been observed and there is no reason to believe that they will stabilise or be diverted in the near future.

Until 1989, the number of immigrants who officially reported the establishment of their permanent residence in Poland oscillated between roughly 1,000 and 1,500 annually. At the end of the 1990s that number reached nearly 10,000 and there were no fewer than 70,000 legal resident aliens believed to be living in Poland by the end of 1997. People from the former Soviet Union, mainly Ukraine, Russia and Belarus, constituted more than half this number. On the other hand, irregular immigrants are here in even greater numbers, among whom Armenians predominate. As yet the numbers are not large relative to the size of local population; however, in my opinion, this is the beginning of an inevitable process and rapidly increasing trends are the best indicators of forthcoming changes in population movements.

Ukrainians represent the most numerous nationality as far as legal immigration in Poland is concerned. Some links between the old Ukrainian minority, which has been in Poland for centuries, and new arrivals are noticeable. However, since in-depth studies concerning "new" Ukrainians are still insufficient, this conclusion is based mainly on the observation of the latter's geographic distribution. Immigrants from Ukraine who obtained permanent residence permits after 1989 are located in areas of traditional Ukrainian settlement and in the regions to which Ukrainians and Lemkos were resettled during Akcja Wisla (Vistula Action) in 1947. Furthermore, the territorial distribution of "new" Ukrainians corresponds to that of Orthodox and Greek Catholic parishes.

Future numerical and behavioural developments in the three prevalent strategies employed by Ukrainians arriving in Poland since 1989 are foreseeable. First, those who are in Poland illegally as seasonal workers or petty-traders with the aim to earn quick money and return home will continue their shuttle mobility for as long as it is profitable and as long as the visa-free regime is in effect. Here it is reasonable to predict fewer petty-traders (which has, in fact already occurred) and more seasonal workers. Second, those who want to settle legally will seek to integrate into the mainstream. With the further development of migrants' networks and institutions, the numbers of Ukrainians granted residence or work permits should grow. There is, however, an element in this group that considers Poland only a transit place on the way to the West. It is possible that the ethnic Ukrainian network plays some role in this strategy since quite large Ukrainian communities exist in Western Europe and North America. Therefore, we may assume that a third strategy, to obtain Polish citizenship (through, for example, marriage) in order to emigrate further west, exists and will continue.

Another very interesting phenomenon is the Vietnamese community in Poland. This is the biggest ethnic group that is unconnected with Poland through history or culture. However, one cannot say that their presence in Poland originated only in 1989. Although the immigration flows to Poland from the early 1960s until the beginning of the 1990s were not statistically significant, one of the then-existent and most visible inflows was of students from certain developing countries, who arrived in Poland under a government-sponsored programme of 'socialist co-operation' or academic exchange. Vietnam was such a country, and Vietnamese students were quite numerous in Poland.

Vietnam started to pursue a more liberal migration policy in 1989. This has led to inflows to Poland and some other countries, not only of students (mostly from privileged families), but also of people seeking a place to work and live. Poland had already been known as a friendly environment by some of them through their friends, acquaintances or family members. This awareness and economic opportunities in post-communist Poland accelerated migratory processes and the formation of a quite sizeable immigrant group.

The new population movements came in the wake of the fall of the communist system also had an enormous impact on labour markets in Poland. Labour migration to Poland is a very recent phenomenon that gathered momentum only in the 1990s. The very fact that there is demand, on the one hand, for highly skilled professionals and, on the other hand, for cheap, low-skilled labour, is indicative of great change on those markets. People have travelled to Poland to work from both the "West" and the "East."

The geography of these flows reflects the global pattern of the division of labour. So far, highly skilled workers come from the West and, to a lesser extent, from Asia; only a small part of the flow from the former Soviet

Union finds employment on Poland's primary labour markets. Flows into this market are highly institutionalised. Immigrants have regulated legal status and are used to supplement the domestic labour force, either as executives in multinationals or through searching for "ethnic niches" as in the case of Asians, for whom setting up a small business, mutual aid and self-employment are instrumental in their occupations on primary markets.

Foreigners from the West are employed mainly in such economic branches as manufacturing, transportation, education and, to some extent, construction. The transfer of skills and knowledge from the West is accompanying the transformation of the Polish economy. Western Europeans and Americans mostly hold managerial functions or are employed as experts, specialists and consultants in all kinds of enterprises, though not often in wholly Polish owned firms.

Vietnamese and Chinese are most often self-employed in small fast food or trading companies. Since 1996 and exclusively due to huge Daewoo investments in Poland, South Koreans are also visible among Asians with executive positions. Contrary to the Vietnamese and Chinese, they are employees of large companies that invest in Poland.

Flows from the "East" (the former Soviet Union and to a lesser degree from Asia) reflect the dynamics of migratory processes that are transforming and will continue to transform temporary entry into settlement. Eastern Europeans prevail as unskilled or skilled manual workers (including artists). Thus even those with work permits have, to date, mainly jobs in the secondary labour market. Nonetheless, they definitely fill some gaps in, and respond to a demand by, local labour markets. Such workers are hired mainly in such sectors as: agriculture and forestry, construction, manufacturing and transportation. In contrast to Western Europeans, Americans and Asians, they are employed most often in state-owned and private, wholly Polish-owned firms.

As far as the future of labour migration to Poland is concerned, I assume that in likely developments in population mobility it is immigrants from the former Soviet Union and Asia who will be the ones with important roles on primary and secondary labour markets. Since the proportion of foreigners from the East with regular legal status is growing, their role on primary labour markets should also gradually increase. Movements of experts and consultants from the West will most probably sharply drop and be based more often on intermittent visits than lengthy stays.

Some part of the salaried migration from the West comprises Polish return migrants, chiefly children of Polish emigrants of the Solidarity or martial law periods. The social, economic and political transformation underway in Poland since 1989 precipitated new migratory behaviours and strategies concerning return to their home country. As previously mentioned, Poles almost always migrated with the idea to come back home. The fact that this pattern was broken in the post-Second World War period and that most post-1945 émigrés did not return, may be explained by the former Polish state migration policy. Now, in this post-communist period, potential returnees are not forced to consider their decision about their possible return to be irrevocable. Therefore, Poland's liberal migration policy and socio-economic upswing has generated a new type of return migration, a type that did not exist during all but the last years of the communist era, namely the *return of innovation*.

A *return of innovation* is probably the most important type of return migration due to successful returnees' possible contribution to their home countries. The transformation of the system caused many successful emigrants who, as small children, had emigrated with their parents from communist Poland to initiate this type of return. This movement is based mainly on a comparison between economic, social and/or career opportunities in Poland versus their adopted countries.

The dynamic relationship between the geopolitical shift and emerging migratory patterns and process proved to be of extreme importance in post-Second World War Poland. Additionally, economic globalisation and the introduction of a market economy and of capital-intensive production and technologies into the Central and Eastern European region after the collapse of European communism disrupted existing social and economic trends and brought about a widespread human movement. This international human traffic has brought three fundamental changes:

- the slow transformation of Poland from one of the biggest sending countries in the CEE region into a country of net-immigration and transit;
- the slow conversion of Poland from a country belonging to the Central and Eastern European migration system into a country that soon may belong simultaneously to two systems and;
- erosion of the Central and Eastern European migration system, possibly leading to its future disintegration.

Indeed, further analysis of population trends in this part of Europe is an alluring prospect for researchers.

References

Castles, S. and Miller, M.J. (1993), *The Age of Migration: International Population Movements in the Modern World*, Macmillan, London.

Iglicka, K. (2000a), 'Mechanisms of migration from Poland before and during the transition period', *Journal of Ethnic and Migration Studies*, vol. 26, no. 1, pp. 61-73.

King, R. and K. Rybaczuk (1993), 'Southern Europe and the international division of labour: from emigration to immigration', in R. King (ed), *The New Geography of European Migrations*, Belharen Press, London.

Kritz, M. and Zlotnik, H. (1992), 'Global Interactions: Migration Systems, Processes and Policies', in M.M. Kritz, L.L. Lim and H. Zlotnik (eds), *International Migration Systems. A Global Approach*, Clarendon Press, Oxford.

Kurcz, Z. (ed) (1997), *Mniejszosci narodowe w Polsce* (National Minorities in Poland), University of Wroclaw Press, Wroclaw.

Kurcz, Z. (2000), 'The German Minority in Poland after 1945', in F.E.I. Hamilton and K. Iglicka (eds), *From Homogeneity to Multiculuralism. Minorities Old and New in Poland*, SSEES, University of London, London.

Kwilecki, A. (1963), 'Mniejszosci narodowe w Polsce Ludowej' (National Minorities in Peoples' Republic), *Kultura i Spoleczenstwo*, no. 4, pp. 87-8.

Massey, D.S. (1999), 'International Migration at the Dawn of the Twenty-first Century: The Role of the State', *Population and Development Review*, vol. 25, no. 2, pp. 303-22.

Massey, D.S., et al. (1993), 'Theories of International Migration: Review and Appraisal', *Population and Development Review*, vol. 19, no. 3, pp. 431-65.

Ociepka, B. (1994), *Niemcy na Dolnym Slasku w latach 1945-1970* (Germans in Lower Silesia, 1945-1970), PWN, Wroclaw.

Okolski, M. (1994), 'Poland', in S. Ardittis (ed), *The Politics of East-West Migration*, St. Martin's Press, New York.

Roczniki Statystyczne (Statistical yearbooks), (various years), GUS (Central Statistical Office), Warsaw.

Bibliography

Alberoni, F. and Baglioni, G. (1965), *L'integrazione dell'immigrato nella societa industriale*, Il Mulino, Bolognia.
Arango, J. (1998a), 'New Migrations, New Theories', in D.S. Massey, J. Arango, G. Hugo, A. Kouaouci, A. Pellegrino and J.E. Taylor (eds), *Worlds in Motion*, Clarendon Press, Oxford.
Arango, J. (1998b), 'Coming to Terms with European Immigration', in D.S. Massey, J. Arango, G. Hugo, A. Kouaouci, A. Pellegrino, J.E. Taylor (eds), *Worlds in Motion*, Clarendon Press, Oxford.
Ascoli, U. (1986), 'Migration of workers and the labour market: is Italy becoming a country of immigration?', in R. Rogers (ed), *Guests come to stay*, Westview, Boulder.
Babinski, G. (2000), 'The Ukrainians in Poland after the Second World War', in F.E.I. Hamilton and K. Iglicka (eds), *From Homogeneity to Multiculturalism. Minorities Old and New in Poland*, SSEES, University of London, London.
Castles, S. (1995), 'How nation-states respond to immigration and ethnic diversity', *New Community*, vol. 3, no. 21, pp. 293-308.
Castles, S. and Miller, M.J. (1993), *The Age of Migration: International Population Movements in the Modern World*, Macmillan, London.
Central Statistical Office, Various years, Warsaw.
Cerase, F. (1977), 'Nostalgia or Disenchantment: Considerations on Return Migration', in S.M. Tomasi and M.H. Engel (eds), *The Italian experience in the United States*, Center for Migration Studies, New York.
Chesnais, J.C. (1993), 'Soviet emigration: Past, Present and Future', in *The changing course of international migration*, OECD, Paris.
Cieslinska, B. (1992), 'Polacy we Wloszech' (Poles in Italy), *Wiadomosci Socjologiczne*, no. 2, pp. 43-61.
Condominas, G. and Pottier, R. (1983), *Les refugies originares de l'Asia du Sud-Est*, Rapport au President de la Republique, la Documentation Francaise.
Cornelius, W. A. (1978), 'Mexican Migration to the United States, Consequences and US Responses', *Migration and Development Monograph*.
Department for Migration and Refugee Affairs' statistics (1999), Ministry of Interior and Administration, Warsaw.
Department of Justice. Immigration and Naturalization Service, United States, 1939-1957 (1957), US Department of Commerce, Government Printing Office, Washington D.C.
Edwards, R.C. (1975), 'The Social Relations of Production in the Firm and Labor Market Structure', in R.C. Edwards, M. Reich and D.M. Gordon (eds), *Labor Market Segmentation*, D.C. Heath, Lexington.

Frejka, T. (1996), *International Migration in Central and Eastern Europe and the Commonwealth of Independent States*, United Nations, New York and Geneva.

German Federal Statistical Office data (1995), various years.

Glabicka, K. and Sakson, B. (1997), 'Imigracja do Polski i obcokrajowcy w Polsce w swietle oficjalnych statystyk' (Immigration and foreigners in Poland in the light of official statistics), *Working Paper*, no. 35, ISS UW, Warsaw.

Glytsos, N. (2000), 'Aspects of Economic Integration of Ethnic Greek Immigrants', paper presented at the IZA Workshop on Ethnic Migrants in Labour Market and Society, Bonn, Germany, 29-31 January.

Golini, A. Gesano, G. and Heins, G. (1991), 'South-North migration with special reference to Europe', *International Migration*, vol. 29, no. 2, pp. 253-277.

Gordon, D.M. (1972), *Theories of Poverty and Underemployment: Orthodox, Radical and Dual Labor Market Perspectives*, D.C. Heath, Lexington.

Government Population Commission (1989) data, Warsaw.

Halik, T. (1995), *Wyniki badan ankietowych prowadzonych w srodowisku imigrantow wietnamskich* (The results of the survey conducted among Vietnamese immigrants), typescript, ISS UW, Warsaw.

Halik, T. (2000), 'The Vietnamese in Poland. Images/Scenes from the Past, Present and Future', in F.E.I. Hamilton and K. Iglicka, *From Homogeneity to Multiculturalism. Minorities Old and New in Poland*, SSEES, University of London, London.

Hamilton, F.E.I. and Iglicka, K. (eds) (2000), *From Homogeneity to Multiculturalism. Minorities Old and New in Poland*, SSEES, University of London, London.

Heffner, K. (1999), 'The Return of Emigrants from Germany to Upper Silesia: Reality and Prospects', in K. Iglicka and K. Sword (eds), *The Challenge of East-West Migration for Poland*, Macmillan, London.

Hryniewicz, J., Jalowiecki, B. and Myne, A. (1992), *The Brain Drain in Poland*, University of Warsaw Press, Warsaw.

Iglicka, K. (1998a), 'Current migratory patterns', in T. Frejka, M. Okolski and K. Sword (eds), *In-depth studies on migration in Central and Eastern Europe: The case of Poland*, UN, New York, Geneva, pp. 57-69.

Iglicka, K. (1998b), *Analiza zachowan migracyjnych na podstawie wynikow badania etnosondazowego migracji zagranicznych w wybranych regionach Polski w latach 1975-1994* (Analysis of migratory behaviors on selected regions of Poland, 1975-1994 – ethnosurvey results), SGH Press, Warsaw.

Iglicka, K. (1998c), 'Are They Fellow Country-Men or Not? The Migration of Ethnic Poles from Kazakhstan to Poland', *International Migration Review*, vol. 32, no. 4 (Winter), pp. 995-1015.

Iglicka, K. (1999a), 'The Economics of the Petty-Trade on the Eastern Polish Border', in K. Iglicka and K. Sword (eds), *The Challenge of East-West Migration for Poland*, Macmillan, St. Martin's, London, New York.

Iglicka, K. (1999b), 'Nomads and Rangers of Central and Eastern Europe', *ISS Working Papers*, no. 32, Warsaw.

Iglicka, K. (2000a), 'Mechanisms of migration from Poland before and during the transition period', *Journal of Ethnic and Migration Studies*, vol. 26, no. 1, pp. 61-73.
Iglicka, K. (2000b), 'Immigrants in Poland – Patterns of Flow', in F.E.I. Hamilton and K. Iglicka (eds), *From Homogeneity to Multiculturalism: Minorities Old and New in Poland*, SSEES, University of London, London.
Iglicka, K. (2000c), 'Ethnic Division on Emerging Foreign Markets in Poland', *Europe-Asia Studies*, vol. 52, no. 7, pp. 1237-1255.
Iglicka, K. (forthcoming a), 'Migration From and Into Poland in the Light of East-West European Migration', *International Migration*.
Iglicka, K. (forthcoming b), 'The Revival of Ethnic Consciousness: a Case of Poland', *Migracje i Spoleczenstwo*, vol. 4, IH PAN, Warsaw.
Iglicka, K., Barsotti, O. and Lecchini, L. (1999), *Recent Development of Migration From Poland to Europe with a Special Emphasis on Italy. Le migrazioni est-ovest. Le unioni miste in Italia*, Universita di Pisa, report no. 131, Pisa.
Iglicka, K., Jazwinska, E., Kepinska, E. and Korys, P. (1997), 'Imigranci w Polsce w swietle badania etnosondazowego' (Immigrants in Poland in the light of ethnosurvey), *Working Paper*, no. 10, ISS UW, Warsaw.
Iglicka, K., Jazwinska, E. and Okolski, M. (1996), 'Wspolczesne migracje zagraniczne ludnosci Polski. Badania za pomoca podejscia etnosondazowego' (Contemporary international migration of Poles. An ethnosurvey study), *Studia Demograficzne*, no. 4, pp. 3-41.
Iglicka, K. and Sword, K. (eds) (1999), *The Challenge of East-West Migration for Poland*, Macmillan, St. Martin's, London, New York.
Informal Labor Market (1995), *Ministry of Labor Press*, Warsaw.
Jagielski, J. (1997), *Status prawny cudzoziemca w Polsce* (Legal status of foreigners in Poland), Warsaw.
Janicki, L. (1995), 'Status mniejszosci narodowych w konstytucjach krajow srodkowo-i wschodnioeuropejskich' (The status of national minorities in constitutions of Central and East European countries), *Przeglad Zachodni*, no. 4, pp. 24-31.
Jedlicki, J. (1999), 'Historical memory as a source of conflicts in Eastern Europe', *Communist and Post Communist Studies*, vol. 32, no. 3, pp. 228-229.
Jerczynski, M. (1999), 'Patterns of Spatial Mobility of Citizens of the Former Soviet Union', in K. Iglicka and K. Sword (eds), *The Challenge of East-West Migration for Poland*, Macmillan, London.
Kersten, K. (1974), *Repatriacja ludnosci Polski po drugiej wojnie swiatowej* (Repatriation of Polish Population after the Second World War), University of Wroclaw Press, Wroclaw.
Khomra, A. (1994), *'Torgova migratsiya ukrainskovo naselennyja v Polshu'* (Petty-trade migration of Ukrainian population to Poland), NISS report (typescript), Kiev.
King, R. and K. Rybaczuk (1993), 'Southern Europe and the international division of labour: from emigration to immigration', in R. King (ed), The New Geography of European Migrations, Belharen Press, London.

Korcelli, P. (1991), 'International Migrations in Europe: Polish Perspectives for the 1990s', *International Migration Review*, vol. 24, no. 2, pp. 1671-1689.
Kosinski, L. (1969), 'Migration of the Population in East-Central Europe, 1939-1955', *Canadian Slavonic Papers*, no. 3, pp. 22-35.
Kotkin, J. (1993), *The Human Races: How Race, Religion and Self-Identity Influence Success in the New Global Economy*, Random House, New York.
Kozlowski, T.K. (1999), 'Migration Flows in the 1990s: Challenges for Entry, Asylum and Integration Policy in Poland', in K. Iglicka and K. Sword (eds), *The Challenge of East-West Migration for Poland*, Macmillan, London.
Kranz, J. (ed) (1998), *Law and Practice of Central European Countries in the Field of National Minorities Protection after 1989*, Center for International Relations, Warsaw.
Kritz, M. and Zlotnik, H. (1992), 'Global Interactions: Migration Systems, Processes and Policies', in M.M. Kritz, L.L. Lim and H. Zlotnik (eds), *International Migration Systems. A Global Approach*, Clarendon Press, Oxford.
Kurcz, Z. (ed) (1997), *Mniejszosci narodowe w Polsce* (National Minorities in Poland), University of Wroclaw Press, Wroclaw.
Kurcz, Z. (2000), 'The German Minority in Poland after 1945', in F.E.I. Hamilton and K. Iglicka (eds), *From Homogeneity to Multiculturalism. Minorities Old and New in Poland*, SSEES, University of London, London.
Kwilecki, A. (1963), 'Mniejszosci narodowe w Polsce Ludowej' (National Minorities in Peoples' Republic), *Kultura i Spoleczenstwo*, no. 4, pp. 87-88.
Latuch, M. (1961), *Repatriacja ludnosci Polski w latach 1955-1960 na tle ruchow wedrowkowych* (Repatriation of Polish population in the light of population mobility in the country), SGPiS Press, Warsaw.
Lee, E.S. (1966), 'A Theory of Migration', *Demography*, no. 3, pp. 5-18.
Lempinski, Z. (1987), *RFN wobec problemow ludnosciowych w stosunkach z Polska, 1970-1985* (Federal Republic of Germany on population in relations with Poland), Slaski Instytut Naukowy, Katowice.
Lukowski, W. (1998), 'A "Pendular Society": Hypotheses Based On In-Depth Interviews and Qualitative Research', in T. Frejka, M. Okolski and K. Sword (eds), *In-Depth Studies on Migration in Central and Eastern Europe: The Case of Poland*, UN, New York and Geneva, pp. 145-153.
Marciniak, T. (2000), 'Armenians in Poland after 1989', in F.E.I. Hamilton and K. Iglicka (eds), *From Homogeneity to Multiculturalism. Minorities Old and New in Poland*, SSEES, University of London, London.
Massey, D.S. (1987), 'The Ethnosurvey in Theory and Practice', *International Migration Review*, vol. 21, no. 4, pp. 1498-1522.
Massey, D.S. (1998), 'Contemporary Theories of International Migration', in D.S. Massey, J. Arango, G. Hugo, A. Kouaouci, A. Pellegrino, J.E. Taylor (eds), *Worlds in Motion*, Clarendon Press, Oxford.
Massey, D.S. (1999), 'International Migration at the Dawn of the Twenty-first Century: The Role of the State', *Population and Development Review*, vol. 25, no. 2, pp. 303-322.

Massey, D.S., et al. (1987), *Return to Aztlan: The social process of International Migration from Western Mexico*, University of California, Berkley.
Massey, D.S., et al. (1993), 'Theories of International Migration: Review and Appraisal', *Population and Development Review*, vol. 19, no. 3, pp. 431-465.
Michalska, A. (1997), 'Pracownicy-migranci jako "nowa" mniejszosc narodowa' (Immigrants-workers as a "new" minority), *Sprawy Narodowosciowe. Seria Nowa*, no. 1, pp. 96-104.
Migration in Central and Eastern Europe – Review (1999), IOM, Geneva.
Mines, R. (1981), 'Developing a Community Tradition of Migration: a Field Study in Rural Zacatecas, Mexico and California Settlement Areas', *US-Mexican Studies*, no. 3, pp. 15-19.
Morokvasic, M. and de Tinguy, A. (1993), 'Between East and West: A New Migratory Space', in H. Rudolph and M. Morokvasic (eds), *Bridging States and Markets: International Migration in the early 1990s*, Sigma, Berlin.
Moynihan, D.P. (1963), *Beyond the Melting Pot*, The M.I.T. Press, Cambridge.
Ociepka, B. (1994), *Niemcy na Dolnym Slasku w latach 1945-1970* (Germans in Lower Silesia, 1945-1970), PWN, Wroclaw.
OECD (1999), *Trends in International Migration*, SOPEMI report, OECD, Paris.
Okolski, M. (1994), 'Poland', in S. Ardittis (ed), *The Politics of East-West Migration*, St. Martin's Press, New York.
Okolski, M. (1995), *Trends in International Migrations. Poland: the 1995 SOPEMI Report*, OECD, Paris.
Okolski, M. (1996), *Trends in International Migrations. Poland: the 1996 SOPEMI Report*, OECD, Paris.
Okolski, M. (1997), 'New migration trends in Central and Eastern Europe in the 1990s', *ISS Working Papers*, no. 4, Warsaw.
Okolski, M. (1998a), 'Regional dimension of international migration in Central and Eastern Europe', *Genus*, vol. LIV, no. 1-2, pp. 11-37.
Okolski, M. (1998b), 'A profile of the communities', in T. Frejka, M. Okolski and K. Sword (eds), *In-depth studies on migration in Central and Eastern Europe: The case of Poland*, UN, New York, Geneva, pp. 189-217.
Okolski, M. (1998c), *Recent trends in international migration – Poland 1998*, SOPEMI report, Paris.
Okolski, M. (1999), 'Recent Migration in Poland: Trends and Causes', in K. Iglicka and K. Sword (eds), *The Challenge of East-West Migration for Poland*, Macmillan, St. Martin's, London, New York.
Patterns and trends in international migration in Western Europe (2000), Luxembourg, European Commission.
Petersen, W. (1966), 'A General Typology of Migration', in C.J. Jansen (ed), *Readings in the Sociology of Migration*, Pergamon Press, Oxford.
Pilch, A. and Zgorniak, M. (eds) (1984), *Emigracja z ziem polskich w czasach nowozytnych i najnowszych* (Emigration from Polish lands in modern and contemporary times), PWN, Warsaw.
Piore, M.J. (1979), *Birds of Passage: Migrant Labor and Industrial Societies*, Cambridge University Press, Cambridge.

Poland – statistical data on migration 1994-1998 (1999), Office for Migration and Refugees, Warsaw.
Polish Border Guard statistics, Various years.
Portes, A. (1981), 'Modes of Structural Incorporation and Present Theories of Labour Immigration', in M.M. Kritz, C.B. Keely and S.M. Tomasi (eds), *Global Trends in Migration*, Center for Migration Studies, New York.
Pries, L. (ed) (1999), *Migration and Transnational Social Spaces*, Ashgate, Aldershot.
Ravenstein, E.G. (1885), 'The Laws of Migration', *Journal of the Royal Statistical Society*, no. 52.
Richmond, A.H. (1984), 'Explaing Return Migration', in D. Kubat (ed), *The Politics of Return. International Return Migration in Europe*, New York: Center for Migration Studies.
Rocznik Demograficzny (Demographic Yearbook) (1998), GUS, Warsaw.
Roczniki Statystyczne (Statistical yearbooks), (various years), GUS (Central Statistical Office), Warsaw.
Rogers, R. (1984), 'Return migration in a comparative perspective', in D. Kubat (ed), *The Politics of Return. International Return Migration in Europe*, Center for Migration Studies, New York.
Romaniszyn, K. (1996), 'Polacy w Grecji' (Poles in Greece), *Studia Polonijne*, vol. 16, pp. 7-98.
Romaniszyn, K. (1997), 'Wspolczesna nielegalna migracja zarobkowa z Polski do Grecji w perspektywie procesu integracji Europy' (Recent illegal income-generating migration from Poland to Greece in the light of the process of European Integration), in J.E. Zamojski (ed), *Migracje i Spoleczenstwo*, vol. 2, pp. 153-163.
Ruch graniczny i wydatki cudzoziemcow w Polsce, 1994-1996 (1997), GUS (Central Statistical Office), Warsaw.
Rudolph, H. and Hillman, F. (1998), 'The Invisible Hand Needs Visible Heads: Managers, Experts and Professionals from Western Countries in Poland', in K. Koser and H. Lutz (eds), *Social Constructions and Social Realities*, Macmillan, London.
Salt, J. (1989), 'A Comparative Overview of International Trends and Types, 1950-80', *International Migration Review*, vol. 15, no. 3, pp. 431-456.
Salt, J. (1996), 'Current trends in international migration in Europe', Council of Europe (paper presented at the 6th Conference of European Ministers responsible for migration affairs), Strasbourg.
Sassen, S. (1988), *The Mobility of Labor and Capital: A Study of International Investment and Labor Flow*, University Press Cambridge, Cambridge.
Slany, K. (1991), 'Emigracja z Polski w latach 1980 do glownych krajow emigracji zamorskiej i kontynentalnej: aspekty demograficzno-spoleczne' (Emigration from Poland to the main countries of destination in the 1980s: demographic and social aspects), *Przeglad Polonijny*, no. 4, pp. 15-36.
Slany, K. (ed) (1997), Emigracyjne orientacje Polakow (Emigrational Orientation of Poles), UJ, Krakow.

Sprawozdanie z badania sondazowego zezwolenia na prace udzielane cudzoziemcom przez wojewodzkie urzedy pracy w okresie 1994-1995 (30 czerwiec), 1995 (1996), Ministry of Labor Press, Warsaw.

Stachanczyk, P. (1998), *Cudzoziemcy. Praktyczny przewodnik do ustawy o cudzoziemcach* (Foreigners. A practical guide for an Alien Law), Warsaw.

Stola, D. (2000), 'New Migrations to Poland: Conditions and Mechanisms of Development', in F.E.I. Hamilton and K. Iglicka (eds), *From Homogeneity to Multiculturalism: Minorities Old and New in Poland*, SSEES, University of London, London.

Stola, D. (forthcoming), 'Migrations in Central Europe: Poland', in C. Wallace and D. Stola (eds), *Central Europe: The New Migration Space*, Macmillan, London.

Stpiczynski, T. (1992), *Polacy w swiecie* (Poles in the World), GUS (Central Statistical Office), Warsaw.

Sword, K. (1999), 'Cross-Border "Suitcase Trade" and the Role of Foreigners in Polish Informal Markets', in K. Iglicka and K. Sword (eds), *The Challenge of East-West Migration for Poland*, Macmillan, London.

Tor, K. (1999), 'Polsko-Wietnamska fikcja malzenska' (Polish-Vietnamese marital fiction), 'Rzeczpospolita', 19 October.

Tsoukala, A. (1999), 'The perception of the "other" and the integration of immigrants in Greece', in A. Geddes and A. Favell (eds), *The Politics of Belonging: Migrants and Minorities in Contemporary Europe*, Ashgate, Aldershot, pp. 109-123.

UNHCR (1993), Population Concern to UNHCR: A Statistical Overview, Geneva.

Walaszek, A. (1984), 'Return Migration from the USA to Poland', in D. Kubat (ed), *The Politics of Return. International Return Migration in Europe*, Center for Migration Studies, New York.

Wallace, C. and Stola, D. (forthcoming) (eds), *Central Europe. The New Migration Space*, Macmillan, London.

Wasilewska-Trenkner, M. (1973), *Ekonomiczno-spoleczne aspekty emigracji z Polski w latach 1960-1965* (Economic and social aspects of emigration from Poland, 1960-1965), WES SGPiS Press, Warsaw.

Zolberg, A.R. (1989), 'The next waves: migration theory for a changing world', *International Migration Review*, no. 23, pp. 403-30.

Index

Act of Employment and Counteracting Unemployment 11, 96
Administrative division 52
Afghanistan 63, 64
Africa 7, 42, 55, 74, 89
Akcja Wisla (Vistula Action) 79, 129
Albanians 49
Aliens Law 11, 59, 70n
Andorra 119
Argentina 17, 19
Armenia 63, 64, 76, 77, 81, 82
Armenians 10, 64, 65, 70n, 83, 86, 87, 93, 116, 127, 129
Asia 2, 6, 7, 42, 55, 74, 89, 100, 105, 114-116, 130, 131
Asylum seekers 10, 50, 83, 85, 129
Athens 45, 50, 51
Aussiedlers 15, 32, 33, 115, 122, 123
Australia 19-22, 24-26, 42, 43, 49, 74
Austria 20, 25, 26, 42, 43, 74, 124, 125

Bangladesh 63, 64
Belarus 6, 59, 60, 62, 64, 70n, 75-77, 79, 82, 100, 129
Belgium 40, 41, 45, 46, 124, 125
Bialystok 21, 22, 45, 61
Border 1, 2, 5, 8, 10, 13, 16, 18, 24, 57-59, 62, 63, 65, 68, 69, 75
  control 1
  crossing points 51n, 65, 70n
  eastern 7, 59, 62, 70n, 83
Brain drain 30, 94, 101, 123
  gain 101
Brazil 19
Buffer zone 5, 7, 10, 70, 128
Bulgarians 49, 64

Canada 17, 19-22, 24-26, 32, 41-43, 45, 48, 49, 74, 81, 82, 89, 110, 124
Caucasus 83
Central and Eastern Europe 3-7, 35, 56, 57, 83, 92, 103, 119-121, 128, 132

Chelm 62
China 64, 76, 100
Chinese 93, 97, 100, 131
Cold-War 4
Communism 105, 107, 109, 120, 122, 124, 129, 132
  collapse 4, 5, 9, 56, 119
  system 7-9, 44, 57, 130
Communist bloc countries 4, 40, 95, 127
Constitution of the Republic of Poland 11, 114n
Council of State 114n
Czech Republic 6, 60, 64, 86

Daewoo 101, 131
Denmark 120
Dual labor market theory 2, 11

East Germany 17-21, 51n, 52n
Economy 1, 2, 4, 5, 9, 33, 36, 42, 44, 47, 51, 57, 59, 88, 101, 103, 104, 114, 126, 131, 132
  gray-sphere 2, 49, 50, 96
  market 4, 9, 41, 49, 51, 95, 132
Egyptians 49
Emigration 3-10, 13-35, 42-44, 46, 47, 50, 51n, 52n, 56, 80, 106, 107, 111, 115n
  direct 14, 15
  indirect 14
Ethnic 4, 11, 14, 33, 36, 46, 79-81, 86, 87, 93, 94, 114n, 122, 128, 130
  claims 15, 33, 123, 125
  diversity 92, 93
  Germans 13, 15, 17, 18, 33, 122
  groups' formation 11, 79, 81, 92, 93, 106, 127, 130
  niches 97, 131
  Poles 18, 23, 36, 70n, 76, 77
Ethnosurvey 34, 35, 124
Europe 2-8, 10, 11, 12n, 32-35, 41-43, 52n, 55-57, 61, 67, 68, 70, 74, 78,

81, 83, 93, 97, 103, 105, 112, 114n, 119-122, 128, 130, 132
Exchange rate 9, 39, 57, 96, 127, 128
Expatriates 11, 104

Family reunification (reunion) 2, 17, 18, 23, 27, 33, 51n
Federal Republic of Germany 15, 23, 24, 32, 43, 52n, 122
Finland 120
First World War 12n, 13, 106
France 17, 19-22, 25, 32, 42, 43, 48, 50, 57, 74, 88, 112

Gdansk 22, 26, 30, 52n
Gdansk Pomerania (the Corridor) 122
Geneva Convention 28
German 16, 18, 20, 21, 23, 32-35, 51n, 52n, 59, 101, 103, 113, 115, 122, 123
  identity 33
  minority 33, 34, 122, 123
  Red Cross 18, 23, 51n
Great Britain 19, 21, 22, 76
Greece 42, 43, 45-47, 49-51, 124-126
Greek Catholic Church 79, 80, 129

Human rights 107
Hybrids 104

Iceland 120
Immigrants 1, 2, 5, 8, 10, 11, 12n, 14, 25, 46, 47, 50, 55, 74, 75, 87-89, 91-95, 101, 102, 105, 109, 112, 126, 129, 131
  exclusion 11, 93
  flow 73
  groups formation 92, 94, 130
  workers 15, 51, 126
Immigration 2, 5-8, 10, 12n, 14, 25, 46, 47, 50, 55, 74, 75, 87-89, 91-95, 101, 102, 105, 109, 112, 126, 129, 131
  registration 51n
India 63, 64
Industrial period 1, 12n
Iraq 63, 64
Israel 16-22, 123
Italy 7, 20, 26, 42, 43, 45-51, 52n, 55, 74, 124-126

Jews 17, 123
Joint ventures 103, 104, 115n

Katowice 20-24, 26, 27, 30, 52n, 53n
Kazakhstan 6, 70n, 76, 77, 82
Kiev 62, 65

Labour 2, 3, 11, 13, 49-51, 57, 60, 70, 75, 78, 94-96, 105, 106, 121, 125, 127, 130
  division 105, 130
  force 94, 95, 104, 405, 131
  market 2, 11, 44, 47-50, 55, 60, 94-97, 101, 105, 106, 121, 125-131
  sector 47
  segmentation 94
  migration 2, 5, 8, 55, 96, 131
Lemkos 79, 80, 127, 129
Liechtenstein 119
Lithuania 34, 59, 60, 62, 64, 70n, 76, 77, 79, 82
Lomza 45
Lubniany 36, 38, 40, 41

Marriages (mixed) 75, 80-83, 87, 89, 114n
Martial law 24, 30, 48-50, 104, 126, 131
Mercantile period 12n
Mexico 57
Migrants 2, 5, 7, 9, 10, 13, 14, 21, 23, 25, 26, 28, 30, 33-43, 46-51, 57, 60, 63, 68, 70, 71n, 73, 80, 83, 88-92, 104, 106, 108-111, 113, 115, 120, 124-127, 130, 131
  categories 14, 36-39
Migration 1-11, 12n, 13-18, 20, 21, 23-29, 33-38, 40-47, 49-51, 51n, 52n, 55, 56, 67, 70, 75, 83, 95, 96, 101, 103-106, 112-114, 115n, 119-121, 124-127, 130, 131
  dynamic process 7, 92, 105, 129
  globalization 6
  managerial 101, 105
  mechanisms 8, 120
  patterns 2, 8, 11, 28, 35, 44, 55, 120
  permanent 51n
  policy 1, 2, 4, 5, 10, 13, 32, 87, 107, 108, 120, 123, 125, 128, 130, 132
  return 11, 46, 106, 108, 109, 112-114, 132
  system 2, 8, 10, 11, 120, 127
    of Central and Eastern Europe 4, 119-121, 127, 128, 132
    of the Nordic countries 120
    of the United Kingdom 120

of Western Europe 4, 7, 119, 121, 122
theory 2, 4, 109
typology 9, 56
Ministry of the Interior 18, 52n
Ministry of Labor and Social Policy 60, 96
Mobility 3-5, 10, 12n, 32, 34, 36, 41, 44, 55-57, 59, 65, 66, 70, 75, 81, 94, 95, 101, 105, 110, 112, 119, 120, 122, 124, 127-131
East-West 7, 128
primitive 10, 55-57, 70, 75, 88, 95, 96, 128
spatial 10, 57, 60, 128
West-East 101, 104
Moldova 6, 63, 64
Monaco 119
Monki 36, 38, 40, 41
Multinational companies 104, 110, 115n

Namyslow 36, 38, 40, 41
Network 49, 62, 70, 75, 80, 81, 88, 103, 106, 126, 128, 130
ethnic 81
theory 2
New economics of labor migration 2
New York Protocol 28
North America 2, 20, 42, 74, 101, 121, 130
Norway 25, 120
Notification by the Government of the Polish People's Republic 23, 26, 52n

October thaw 122
Opole 20-24, 26, 27, 30, 52n, 114
Orthodox Church 79, 80, 129

Pakistan 63, 64, 120
Peripheries 46
Passport policy 15, 28, 43
Perlejewo 36, 38, 40, 41
Permanent residence address 16, 51n, 74
Permanent residence permit 10, 71n, 74-79, 83, 87-92, 129
Permission 34, 51n, 55, 75, 79, 122, 129
for fixed-time residence 74, 77
for settlement 74, 77
Petty-traders 37, 43, 55, 57, 60, 61, 65, 66, 71n, 75, 81, 96, 128-130
Podlaskie 35, 36

Polish Church 48
citizenship 18, 23, 24, 51n, 52n, 74, 75, 77, 81, 88, 113, 114, 130
consulate 75
Czechoslovak treaty 16
embassy 48, 52n
heritage 23
nationality 18, 24
Soviet agreement 16, 70n
Post-industrial period 1
Potsdam Agreement 16
Protocol Provision 23, 26
Prussia 35
Przemysl 45, 61
Pull-push framework 2

Refugees 2, 3, 7, 12, 28, 47, 48, 50, 72n, 76-79, 83, 86, 97, 117, 120, 126
Regained Territories 18, 23
Repatriates 18, 19, 23
Repatriation 4, 13, 17, 18, 53, 70, 75, 127
agreement 17
of ethnic Poles 18, 70
process 77, 127
resolution 76, 77
visa 75, 77
Return of innovation 11, 109, 110, 132
Romanians 49, 64
Rome 45, 49, 51
Russia 6, 36, 59, 60, 64, 70n, 76, 77, 79, 82, 100, 129

San Marino 119
Scandinavia 20
Second World War 3, 8, 12n, 13-15, 17, 27, 79, 106, 111, 122, 123, 132
Slovakia 6, 60, 64
Solidarity period 30, 131
South America 2, 42
South Koreans 100, 101, 131
Soviet authorities 76
Soviet Union 5, 6, 10, 33, 55, 57-62, 70n, 95-97, 105, 114n, 120, 126-129, 131
Spätaussiedler 113, 115
Sri Lanka 63, 64
Sweden 25, 32, 42, 74, 120
Switzerland 25, 57, 119

Trans-border activities 63

Transformation 8, 11, 12n, 32, 34, 101, 104, 123, 131, 132
  economic 4, 9, 28, 44, 55, 105, 110, 111, 124-126, 131
  of the system 44, 132
  social 50, 110, 111, 124-126, 131
  political 44, 55, 110, 111, 119, 124-126, 131
Transition 7-9, 11, 13, 15, 28-30, 32, 39, 41, 42, 44, 45, 56, 96, 103-105, 108-110, 113, 121, 123-125
Tsarist authorities 76

U.S. Immigration Act 94
Ukraine 6, 34, 59, 60, 62, 64, 75-77, 79, 82, 100, 127-129
Ukrainian minority 79, 123
Ukrainians 10, 17, 60, 63, 65, 78-81, 87, 93, 123, 127, 129, 130
United Kingdom 42, 43, 74, 82, 100, 120
United States (USA) 13, 32, 42, 43, 74, 81, 82, 100, 120

USSR 5, 6, 13, 16-19, 42, 57, 60-63, 65, 68, 70n, 74, 76, 80, 82, 89

Vietnam 64, 75-77, 82, 87-90, 100, 130
Vietnamese 10, 87, 88, 93, 97, 100, 130, 131
Visa-free movement 59, 70, 130
Visa-rule list 10
Voivod Labour Office 96
Voivodships 19, 20, 23, 51n, 52n, 75, 78
Volksliste 122

Warsaw 11, 21, 22, 26, 30, 46, 61, 68, 69, 88, 112, 113, 119
Warsaw Bazaar 61-62
West Germany 18, 19, 23, 24, 26-28, 34, 51n, 52n, 122
Work permits 25, 70n, 71n, 75, 76, 78, 81, 87, 94, 96, 97-103, 105, 130, 131
World system theory 2

Yugoslavia 5, 6, 64, 83